# PYTHON MAGIC: TURN IDEAS INTO CODE WITH EASE

*Introduction: Welcome to Python Magic*

## The Goal Of This Book

**H**ave you ever imagined conjuring up solutions to real-world problems with just a few lines of code? Have you dreamed of turning complex ideas into reality with nothing more than a keyboard and your creativity? Welcome to  Python Magic: Turn Ideas into Code with Ease, where learning Python becomes an adventure filled with discovery, empowerment, and fun.

This book is designed to transform the way you approach programming. With a focus on simplicity, creativity, and practicality, it provides the tools and knowledge to help you bring your ideas to life, one line of code at a time.

### Why Python is Perfect for Beginners

Python isn't just a programming language; it's a gateway to endless possibilities. Known for its easy-to-read syntax and versatility, Python is the ideal choice for beginners. It's simple enough for someone with no prior experience and powerful enough to tackle advanced problems.

Whether you want to automate daily tasks, build games, analyze data, or create visually stunning charts, Python has you covered. Its gentle learning curve and vast ecosystem make it the perfect starting point for anyone stepping into the world of coding.

### How This Book Makes Learning Python Fun and Simple

Let's face it: learning programming can sometimes feel daunting. But not here! Python Magic is crafted to make the learning process exciting and engaging. Here's what makes this book special:

- **Simplicity** : Complex concepts are broken down into bite-sized, easy-to-understand lessons.
- **Fun** : Interactive exercises, relatable examples, and playful projects keep you motivated and entertained.
- **Practicality** : Each chapter is packed with real-world applications to ensure that you're not just learning but also building skills you can use immediately.
- **Creativity** : Python is a tool for makers and dreamers, and this book helps you harness its power to turn your ideas into reality.

### A Journey of Discovery Awaits

The magic of Python is that it makes the impossible possible. Together, we'll unlock the secrets of this incredible language. From your first "Hello, World!" to building impressive projects, you'll discover the joys of programming one spellbinding step at a time.

So grab your wand (or, in this case, your keyboard) and get ready to embark on an unforgettable adventure. Welcome to the world of Python Magic !

# *Python Installation*

## Tools And Setup

Welcome to the exciting journey of learning Python! Before we dive into writing code, we need to set up our tools. Think of this chapter as preparing your workspace before starting a magical craft. Here, you'll learn how to install Python, set up a coding environment, and write your very first Python program.

### Installing Python

Python is free and open-source, which means you can download and use it without any cost. Follow these steps to install Python on your computer:

## For Windows:

1. Visit the official Python website: [https://www.python.org/] (https://www.python.org/).

2. Click on the **Downloads** section and choose the latest version for Windows.

3. Run the downloaded installer.

4. During installation, check the box that says *"Add Python to PATH"** (this is very important).

5. Follow the prompts and complete the installation.

## For Macos:

1. macOS usually comes with Python pre-installed, but it might be an older version. To get the latest version:

2. Go to [https://www.python.org/](https://www.python.org/).

3. Download the latest version for macOS.

4. Run the installer and follow the instructions.

## For Linux:

1. Most Linux distributions include Python by default. To check, open a terminal and type:

```
python3 --version
```

2. If Python is not installed, you can use your package manager. For example, on Ubuntu:

```
sudo apt update
sudo apt install python3
```

### Setting Up Your Coding Environment

Once Python is installed, you need a place to write and run your code. Here are some popular options:

### IDLE (Integrated Development and Learning Environment)

- IDLE comes bundled with Python. It's simple and great for beginners.

- To open IDLE:

  - On Windows: Search for "IDLE" in the Start menu.
  - On macOS/Linux: Type `idle3` in the terminal.

- **Features**: Syntax highlighting, an interactive shell, and a basic editor.

### Visual Studio Code (VS Code)

- A powerful and versatile code editor.

- Download it from [https://code.visualstudio.com/](https://code.visualstudio.com/).

- Install the **Python extension** for better support.
- Create a new file with a `.py` extension and start coding!

## Jupyter Notebooks

- Best for interactive coding and data visualization.
- Install it using pip:

```
pip install notebook
```

- Run it by typing:

```
jupyter notebook
```

- A web-based interface will open where you can write and run Python code in cells.

### Writing and Running Your First Python Program

Now that your tools are ready, let's write your first Python program. This is the programming equivalent of casting your first spell simple, yet magical!

# Step 1: Open Your Editor
  - If you're using IDLE, open the editor and create a new file.
  - If you're using VS Code, create a new file with a `.py` extension (e.g., `hello.py`).
  - If you're using Jupyter Notebook, create a new notebook.
# Step 2: Write Your Code
Type the following code:

```
print("Hello, Python!")
```

### Step 3: Run Your Code
  - In IDLE: Press `F5` or go to Run > Run Module .

- In VS Code: Right-click and select Run Python File in Terminal .
- In Jupyter Notebook: Press `Shift + Enter`.

You should see the message `Hello, Python!` appear. Congratulations—you just wrote and executed your first Python program!

### Exercise: Your Turn to Code

Now it's time for you to practice. Create a Python program that:

1. Prints your name.

2. Prints your favourite hobby.

### Example Output:

```
My name is Rajesh.
My favourite hobby is writing.
```

Write your code, run it, and enjoy the thrill of creating something on your own. You're off to a magical start!

# PART 01
# FOUNDATIONS
# OF PYTHON

*Chapter 1: Python Basics*

Welcome to the foundations of Python, where the magic begins! This chapter is your gateway to understanding Python's core concepts, from its unique characteristics to the essentials of writing clean and readable code. Each topic is paired with exercises to ensure you not only read but also practice and master these basics.

## What Is Python?

Python is a high-level, versatile programming language that emphasizes readability and simplicity. Created by Guido van Rossum and named after the comedy series Monty Python's Flying Circus, Python has become one of the most popular programming languages in the world. But what makes it so special?

Python's charm lies in its **versatility** you can use it to accomplish almost anything! Here are some examples of what you can do with Python:

## 1. Software Development

Python is widely used for building software applications, from desktop tools to enterprise systems. With frameworks like PyQt and Kivy, you can create user-friendly graphical interfaces for your programs.

## 2. Web Development

Python powers dynamic websites and web applications. Frameworks like Django and Flask make it easy to build robust and scalable web projects. Did you know popular platforms like Instagram and Pinterest use Python behind the scenes?

## 3. Data Analysis And Visualization

Python is a favourite among data scientists. With libraries like pandas, NumPy, and matplotlib, you can process, analyze, and visualize large datasets. It's the go-to tool for creating insightful reports and dashboards.

## 4. Machine Learning And Artificial Intelligence

Python is at the heart of AI and machine learning innovations. Frameworks like TensorFlow and PyTorch allow you to build predictive models, create chatbots, and even design autonomous systems.

## 5. Game Development

Python is used in the gaming industry to create simple games or even prototype complex ones. Libraries like Pygame provide tools for developing engaging 2D games.

## 6. Mathematics And Scientific Computing

Python simplifies complex mathematical problems. With libraries like SymPy and SciPy, you can solve equations, simulate experiments, and analyze results with ease.

## 7. System Scripting

Automate repetitive tasks with Python! Whether it's renaming multiple files, organizing directories, or managing servers, Python scripts save time and effort.

**Key Features of Python:**
- **Ease of Use** : Python's syntax is straightforward, making it beginner-friendly.
- **Versatility** : Python is used in web development, data science, artificial intelligence, automation, and more.
- **Large Community** : A supportive community means tons of resources, libraries, and frameworks at your disposal.

**Why Python Stands Out:**

**1.   Dynamic Typing** : Unlike languages such as Java or C ++, Python doesn't require you to specify variable types. For example, you can simply write:

```
x = 10   Python understands this is an integer
x = "Hello"   Now it's a string, no problem!
```

**2.   Extensive Libraries** : Python comes with a standard library that can handle tasks from web scraping (BeautifulSoup) to machine learning (TensorFlow).

**3.   Cross-Platform Compatibility** : Code written in Python can run seamlessly on different operating systems with little or no modification.

**Exercise:**

Research and write down three unique features of Python compared to other programming languages.

- Example: Python's emphasis on readability makes it ideal for collaboration and education.

## Understanding Syntax And Indentation

Python's clean syntax is one of its most appealing features. Unlike many languages, Python uses indentation to define blocks of code. This enforces readability and eliminates the need for braces (`{}`) or semicolons (`;`).

**Example of Proper Syntax:**

```
if True:
    print("This is properly indented.")
```

**Common Pitfalls:**

- **Incorrect Indentation** : All lines within the same block must have the same level of indentation.
- **Mixing Tabs and Spaces** : Stick to one type of indentation, preferably spaces.

**Exercise:** Rewrite the following snippet to follow Python's indentation rules:
```
if True:
print("Fix this indentation")
    print("Make it consistent")
```

## Variables And Data Types

In Python, **variables** act as containers for storing data. Think of variables as labeled boxes where you can put different types of items, such as numbers, text, or collections of data. Python is incredibly flexible, making it easy to work with various **data types**.

## Common Data Types In Python

Here are the essential data types you'll encounter in Python, along with their real-world uses and examples:

1. **Integers**:
   These are whole numbers, like 42 or -10. Perfect for counting or performing arithmetic.

```
age = 25  # Storing an integer
print(age) # Output: 25
```

2. **Floats**:
   These represent decimal numbers, like 3.14. Useful for precise calculations.

```
pi = 3.14 # Storing a floating-point number
print(pi) # Output: 3.14
```

3. **Strings**:
   Strings are sequences of characters enclosed in quotes. They're used for handling text.

```
name = "Alice"  # Storing a string
print(name) # Output: Alice
```

4. **Booleans**:
   These are logical values: True or False. They're perfect for making decisions in your programs.

```
is_student = True  # Storing a Boolean value
print(is_student) # Output: True
```

5. **Lists**:
   Lists are ordered collections of items. You can store

anything, from numbers to strings, in a list.

```
hobbies = ["reading", "cycling", "painting"] # A list of
hobbies
print(hobbies)
# Output: ['reading', 'cycling', 'painting']
```

6. **Dictionaries**:

Dictionaries store data as key-value pairs, making it easy to organize and retrieve related data.

```
profile = {"name": "Alice", "age": 25, "hobby": "cycling"} #
A dictionary
print(profile)
# Output: {'name': 'Alice', 'age': 25, 'hobby': 'cycling'}
```

# Dynamic Typing In Python

Python allows you to change the type of data a variable holds. For example:

```
x = 10    # Initially an integer
x = "Hello" # Now a string
print(x)   # Output: Hello
```

This flexibility is one of the reasons Python is so beginner-friendly.

### Example: Mixing Data Types in Lists

Python allows you to mix data types within a list.

```
mixed_list = [25, "Alice", True, 3.14]
print(mixed_list)
# Output: [25, 'Alice', True, 3.14]
```

## Assigning Multiple Variables

**Definition:**

Assigning multiple variables allows you to assign values to multiple variables in a single line.

**Example:**

```
# Assigning multiple variables
x, y, z = 10, 20, 30
print(x) # Output: 10
print(y) # Output: 20
print(z) # Output: 30

# Assigning the same value to multiple variables
a = b = c = 100
print(a, b, c)
# Output: 100 100 100
```

**Key Points:**

- You can assign different values to multiple variables in one line.
- You can assign the same value to multiple variables.

## Global Variables

**Definition:**

A **global variable** is a variable declared outside a function, making it accessible throughout the program.

**Explanation:**

- Variables declared inside a function are **local variables**.
- Use the global keyword to modify global variables inside a function.

**Example:**

```
# Global variable
global_var = 10

def my_function():
    global global_var  # Accessing global variable
    global_var += 5
    print("Inside function:", global_var)

my_function()  # Output: Inside function: 15
print("Outside function:", global_var)
# Output: Outside function: 15
```

**Key Points:**

- Global variables are accessible from any part of the program.
- Use the global keyword inside functions to modify a global variable.

**Exercise: Play with Variables**

1. Declare variables to store your name, age, and a list of your favourite foods.
2. Create a dictionary to represent a person's profile with keys for name, age, and is_student.

Write a program that swaps the values of two variables and prints the result.

---

**Exercise:**

Create a program that assigns and prints variables of different data types. Include at least one example of a list and a dictionary.

---

## *Comments and Readability*

Writing code is not just about making it work; it's about making it easy to understand, debug, and improve. This is where **comments** come in they act as signposts, explaining your thought process and making your code easier for others (and your future self) to follow.

### What Are Comments?

In Python, comments are lines in your code that the interpreter ignores during execution. They're like sticky notes that tell readers why the code exists, what it does, or how it works.

---

### How to Write Comments in Python

1. **Single-Line Comments**:
   Use the # symbol for single-line comments.

```
# This prints a welcome message to the user
print("Welcome to Python programming!")
```

2. **Multi-Line Comments**:
   Use triple quotes (""" or ''') for comments spanning multiple lines.

```
This program calculates the area of a rectangle.
Length and width are provided by the user.

length = 10
width = 5
print("Area:", length * width)
```

---

### Why Use Comments?

Comments are more than just helpful notes; they're a powerful tool for creating clean, maintainable, and professional-grade code.

- **Explain the Purpose of Complex Code**:
  When working with algorithms or intricate logic, comments clarify what the code is doing.

```python
# Check if the input number is a prime number
def is_prime(num):
    for i in range(2, num):
        # If divisible, it's not a prime number
        if num % i == 0:
            return False
    return True
```

- **Temporarily Disable Parts of Code**:
  During debugging or testing, you can comment out certain lines without deleting them.

```python
# print("Debugging mode: Variable values") # Disabled for production
print("Program is running smoothly.")
```

- **Document Code for Collaboration**:
  Well-commented code helps teams collaborate effectively. Others can understand and modify the code without additional explanations.

## Best Practices for Comments

1. **Be Concise Yet Clear**:
   Avoid overly detailed comments. Focus on the *why*, not the *how* (the code itself explains the *how*).

```python
# Calculate the square of the number
result = number ** 2
```

2. **Update Comments**:
   Always update comments when the corresponding code changes to avoid confusion.

3. **Avoid Obvious Comments**:

Don't state the obvious; instead, add value with your comments.

**Avoid:**

```
# Add 5 to x
x = x + 5
```

**Better:**

```
# Adjust the score for bonus points
x = x + 5
```

## Examples of Good and Bad Comments

**Bad Comment:**

```
# Create a list
fruits = ["apple", "banana", "cherry"]
```

**Good Comment:**

```
# List of fruits available in the inventory
fruits = ["apple", "banana", "cherry"]
```

**Bad Comment:**

```
# Loop through the list
for fruit in fruits:
    print(fruit)
```

**Good Comment:**

```
# Print each fruit from the inventory list
for fruit in fruits:
    print(fruit)
```

## Exercise: Practice Writing Comments

1. Write a program that calculates the factorial of a number. Add comments to explain each step.
2. Create a program that reads a file and prints its content. Add comments to explain file handling.

3. Open a program you've written before and add meaningful comments to make it more readable.

---

By using comments effectively, you not only make your code more readable but also demonstrate professionalism and attention to detail.

When in doubt, remember: Comments are a conversation between you and anyone reading your code. So, make them count!

---

**Exercise:**

Add comments to the following code snippet explaining each step:

```
a = 10    Assign 10 to a
b = 20    Assign 20 to b
sum = a + b    Calculate the sum of a and b
print(sum)    Display the result
```

---

By the end of this chapter, you'll have a solid understanding of Python's basics. These foundational skills will be your toolkit as we journey deeper into the magical world of Python programming!

# CHAPTER 2: WORKING WITH NUMBERS AND TEXT

**W**elcome to Chapter 2, where we explore Python's ability to handle numbers and text—the foundation of most programs. You'll learn about basic arithmetic, string manipulation, and how to interact with users through input and output. Let's dive into these exciting topics with practical examples and hands-on exercises!

## *Basic Arithmetic and Operators*

Python excels at performing calculations. You can use it as a calculator to perform addition, subtraction, multiplication, division, and more. Here are the basic arithmetic operators in Python.

## 1. Addition (+)

The + operator is used to add two numbers.

**Examples:**

```
# Example 1: Adding integers
x = 10
y = 5
result = x + y
print(result) # Output: 15

# Example 2: Adding floats
a = 3.2
b = 2.8
result = a + b
print(result) # Output: 6.0
```

## 2. Subtraction (-)

The - operator is used to subtract one number from another.

**Examples:**

```
# Example 1: Subtracting integers
x = 15
y = 7
result = x - y
print(result) # Output: 8

# Example 2: Subtracting floats
a = 5.5
b = 2.2
result = a - b
print(result) # Output: 3.3
```

## 3. Multiplication (*)

The * operator is used to multiply two numbers.

**Examples:**

```
# Example 1: Multiplying integers
x = 6
y = 4
result = x * y
print(result) # Output: 24

# Example 2: Multiplying floats
a = 1.5
b = 4.2
result = a * b
print(result) # Output: 6.3
```

## 4. Division (/)

The / operator is used to divide one number by another. It always returns a float, even if the numbers are integers.

**Examples:**

```
# Example 1: Dividing integers
x = 20
y = 4
result = x / y
print(result) # Output: 5.0

# Example 2: Dividing floats
a = 7.5
b = 2.5
result = a / b
print(result) # Output: 3.0
```

## 5. Floor Division (//)

The // operator performs division but truncates the result to the nearest whole number (floored value).

**Examples:**

```
# Example 1: Floor division with integers
x = 17
```

```
y = 4
result = x // y
print(result) # Output: 4

# Example 2: Floor division with floats
a = 9.8
b = 3.2
result = a // b
print(result) # Output: 3.0
```

## 6. Modulus (%)

The % operator returns the remainder of a division.

**Examples:**

```
# Example 1: Modulus with integers
x = 17
y = 4
result = x % y
print(result) # Output: 1

# Example 2: Modulus with floats
a = 9.8
b = 3.2
result = a % b
print(result) # Output: 0.2
```

## 7. Exponentiation (**)

The ** operator raises one number to the power of another.

**Examples:**

```
# Example 1: Exponentiation with integers
x = 2
y = 3
result = x ** y
print(result) # Output: 8
```

```
# Example 2: Exponentiation with floats
a = 3.5
b = 2
result = a ** b
print(result) # Output: 12.25
```

## Summary Of Arithmetic Operators

| Operator | Description | Example | Result |
|---|---|---|---|
| + | Addition | 10 + 5 | 15 |
| - | Subtraction | 10 - 5 | 5 |
| * | Multiplication | 10 * 5 | 50 |
| / | Division (returns float) | 10 / 5 | 2.0 |
| // | Floor Division | 10 // 3 | 3 |
| % | Modulus (remainder) | 10 % 3 | 1 |
| ** | Exponentiation (power) | 2 ** 3 | 8 |

**Points to Note**

1. **Order of Operations (PEMDAS)**: Python follows the standard order of operations:
   - Parentheses > Exponents > Multiplication/ Division > Addition/Subtraction.
2. result = 2 + 3 * 4 # Output: 14
3. result = (2 + 3) * 4 # Output: 20

4. **Division by Zero**: Dividing by zero will raise a ZeroDivisionError.

5. print(10 / 0) # Raises ZeroDivisionError

---

## Strings and String Operations

*Strings in Python are sequences of characters enclosed in quotes. They are one of the most fundamental data types and are incredibly versatile. Whether you're working with single-line text or multi-line paragraphs, Python makes handling strings simple yet powerful with numerous built-in operations and methods.*

Let's explore what you can do with strings and how to master string operations in Python.

---

### What Are Strings?

Strings are enclosed in single quotes ('), double quotes ("), or triple quotes (''' or """) for multi-line strings.

Examples:

```
# Single-line strings
greeting = 'Hello'
name = "Alice"

# Multi-line strings
multi_line = """This is
a multi-line string."""
```

---

### String Operations

Python offers a variety of ways to manipulate strings. Let's dive into the key operations with examples:

---

## 1. Concatenation: Combine Strings

Use the + operator to join two or more strings.

```
first_name = "Rajesh"
last_name = "Patil"
full_name = first_name + " " + last_name
print(full_name) # Output: Rajesh Patil
```

## 2. Repetition: Repeat Strings

Multiply a string using the * operator.

```
name = "Python "
print(name * 3) # Output: Python Python Python
```

## 3. Indexing and Slicing: Access Parts of a String

Strings are indexed starting from 0 (left to right) and -1 (right to left). You can also extract substrings using slicing.

```
message = "Hello, Python!"
print("First character:", message[0])  # Output: H
print("Last character:", message[-1]) # Output: !
print("Substring:", message[7:13])    # Output: Python
```

## 4. String Methods

Python strings come with many built-in methods to perform specific tasks.

### 1. Case Modification

- **str.upper()**: Converts all characters to uppercase.
- print("python".upper()) # Output: PYTHON
- **str.lower()**: Converts all characters to lowercase.

print("PYTHON".lower()) # Output: python

- **str.capitalize()**: Capitalizes the first character of the string.

print("python programming".capitalize()) # Output: Python programming

- **str.title()**: Converts the first character of each word to uppercase.

print("python programming".title()) # Output: Python Programming

- **str.swapcase()**: Swaps the case of each character.
  print("PyThOn".swapcase()) # Output: pYtHoN

## 2. Searching and Finding

- **str.find(substring)**: Returns the index of the first occurrence of a substring, or -1 if not found.

print("hello world".find("world")) # Output: 6

- **str.index(substring)**: Like find(), but raises an error if the substring is not found.

print("hello world".index("world")) # Output: 6

- **str.startswith(prefix)**: Returns True if the string starts with the specified prefix.

print("hello".startswith("he")) # Output: True

- **str.endswith(suffix)**: Returns True if the string ends with the specified suffix.

print("hello".endswith("lo")) # Output: True

- **str.count(substring)**: Counts the occurrences of a substring in the string.

print("banana".count("a")) # Output: 3

## 3. Modifying Strings

- **str.strip()**: Removes leading and trailing whitespace.

print(" hello ".strip()) # Output: hello

- **str.lstrip()**: Removes leading (left) whitespace.

print(" hello".lstrip()) # Output: hello

- **str.rstrip()**: Removes trailing (right) whitespace.

```
print("hello ".rstrip()) # Output: hello
```

- **str.replace(old, new)**: Replaces all occurrences of old with new.

```
print("hello world".replace("world", "Python")) # Output:
hello Python
```

## 4. Splitting and Joining

- **str.split(delimiter)**: Splits the string into a list of substrings based on a delimiter.

```
print("apple,banana,cherry".split(",")) # Output: ['apple',
'banana', 'cherry']
```

- **str.rsplit(delimiter)**: Like split(), but starts splitting from the right.

```
print("apple,banana,cherry".rsplit(",", 1)) # Output:
['apple,banana', 'cherry']
```

- **str.splitlines()**: Splits the string into a list of lines.

```
print("line1\nline2\nline3".splitlines()) # Output: ['line1',
'line2', 'line3']
```

- **str.join(iterable)**: Joins elements of an iterable into a single string with the string as a separator.

```
print(", ".join(["apple", "banana", "cherry"])) # Output:
apple, banana, cherry
```

## 5. Checking String Content

- **str.isalpha()**: Returns True if all characters are alphabetic.

```
print("hello".isalpha()) # Output: True
```

- **str.isdigit()**: Returns True if all characters are digits.

```
print("12345".isdigit()) # Output: True
```

- **str.isalnum()**: Returns True if all characters are alphanumeric.

print("hello123".isalnum()) # Output: True

- **str.isspace()**: Returns True if all characters are whitespace.

print(" ".isspace()) # Output: True

- **str.islower()**: Returns True if all characters are lowercase.

print("hello".islower()) # Output: True

- **str.isupper()**: Returns True if all characters are uppercase.

print("HELLO".isupper()) # Output: True

- **str.istitle()**: Returns True if the string is title-cased.

print("Hello World".istitle()) # Output: True

## 6. Encoding and Formatting

- **str.format()**: Formats the string using placeholders.

print("My name is {name} and I am
{age}.".format(name="Alice", age=25))

- # Output: My name is Alice and I am 25.
- **str.encode()**: Encodes the string into bytes using the specified encoding.

print("hello".encode()) # Output: b'hello'

## 7. Miscellaneous Methods

- **str.zfill(width)**: Pads the string with zeros on the

left to fill the specified width.

```
print("42".zfill(5))  # Output: 00042
```

- **str.center(width)**: Centers the string within the specified width.

```
print("hello".center(10)) # Output: ' hello '
```

- **str.ljust(width)**: Left-aligns the string within the specified width.

```
print("hello".ljust(10)) # Output: 'hello    '
```

- **str.rjust(width)**: Right-aligns the string within the specified width.

```
print("hello".rjust(10)) # Output: '    hello'
```

**Examples:**

```
text = " python programming "
print(text.strip())      # Removes leading/trailing spaces:
'python programming'
print(text.upper())      # Converts to uppercase: 'PYTHON
PROGRAMMING'
print(text.replace("python", "Python")) # Replaces a
substring: ' Python programming '
```

## What You Can Do with Strings

Beyond the basic operations, Python offers a vast array of possibilities for working with strings:

### 1. Iterate Over Strings

Use loops to process each character in a string.

```
for char in "Python":
    print(char)
```

### 2. Modify Case

```
text = "Python Programming"
print(text.lower()) # Output: python programming
print(text.title()) # Output: Python Programming
```

## 3. Strip Whitespace

```
text = "  Hello, Python!  "
print(text.strip())  # Output: Hello, Python!
```

## 4. Find and Replace

```
text = "Python is fun"
print(text.find("fun"))      # Output: 10
print(text.replace("fun", "awesome")) # Output: Python is
awesome
```

## 5. Split and Join Strings

Break a string into parts using split() and combine them using join().

```
text = "apple,banana,cherry"
fruits = text.split(",")
print(fruits) # Output: ['apple', 'banana', 'cherry']

joined = " ".join(fruits)
print(joined) # Output: apple banana cherry
```

## 6. Format Strings

Use placeholders to create dynamic strings.

```
name = "Alice"
age = 25
print(f"My name is {name} and I am {age} years old.")
# Output: My name is Alice and I am 25 years old.
```

## Key Takeaways

1. Strings are sequences of characters enclosed in quotes.
2. Python provides powerful tools for creating, modifying, and analysing strings.
3. Common operations include concatenation, repetition, indexing, slicing, and string methods.
4. String methods like strip(), upper(), and replace() make working with text easier.
5. Advanced operations like splitting, joining, and formatting add flexibility to string handling.

## Practice Exercises

1. Write a program to reverse a given string.
2. Count the number of vowels in a user-provided string.
3. Create a script to check if a string is a palindrome.
4. Extract the domain name from an email address using slicing and methods.
5. Write a program that replaces all spaces in a string with underscores.

With these tools and techniques, you're ready to handle text like a pro in Python. Strings are everywhere in programming—from processing user input to generating output—so mastering them will significantly boost your coding skills.

---

**Exercise:** Write a program that asks the user for their name and prints it in uppercase, lowercase, and reversed.

---

## Input and Output in Python

Python allows you to interact with users by taking input and displaying output using the `input()` function and `print()` statement.

**Examples:**

**Example 1: Simple Input and Output**

```
#Asking for user input
name = input("What is your name? ")
print("Hello, " + name + "!")
```

**Example 2: Handling Numerical Input**

```
# Taking numerical input
age = int(input("Enter your age: "))
print("You are " + str(age) + " years old.")
```

**Example 3: Formatting Output**

```
#Using formatted strings
price = 49.99
print(f"The price of the item is ${price:.2f}.")
```

**Exercise:**
Create a program that takes user input for their age and
calculates the year they were born.

---

*By the end of this chapter, you'll be equipped to perform
calculations, manipulate text, and create interactive
programs with ease. Keep practicing the examples and
exercises to solidify your understanding!*

◆ ◆ ◆

# Casting in Python

C asting refers to the process of converting one data type into another in Python. It is useful when you need to explicitly change the type of a variable to match the requirements of an operation or function.

Python supports **implicit casting** (automatically done by Python) and **explicit casting** (done manually using built-in functions).

## 1. Implicit Casting

Python automatically converts one data type to another whenever required, without explicit instructions from the programmer. This usually happens when combining compatible data types.

**Example of Implicit Casting:**

```
x = 5    # Integer
y = 2.5   # Float
result = x + y # Integer + Float
print(result)  # Output: 7.5
print(type(result)) # Output: <class 'float'>
```

In this example:

- Python automatically converts the integer x into a float to perform the addition because the result involves a float.

## 2. Explicit Casting

Explicit casting is when the programmer manually converts one data type into another using Python's built-in functions. It is required when data types are incompatible or when precision is needed.

**Built-in Casting Functions:**

| Function | Description | Example |
|----------|-------------|---------|
| int() | Converts to an integer, truncating decimals. | int(3.7) → 3 |
| float() | Converts to a floating-point number. | float(5) → 5.0 |
| str() | Converts to a string. | str(123) → '123' |
| list() | Converts to a list. | list((1, 2, 3)) → [1, 2, 3] |
| tuple() | Converts to a tuple. | tuple([1, 2, 3]) → (1, 2, 3) |
| set() | Converts to a set. | set([1, 2, 3]) → {1, 2, 3} |
| bool() | Converts to a Boolean. | bool(0) → False |

## Examples of Explicit Casting

**Converting Float to Integer**

```
x = 3.14
y = int(x) # Explicitly casting float to int
```

```
print(y)   # Output: 3
```

## Converting Integer to String

```
x = 42
y = str(x) # Explicitly casting int to string
print(y)   # Output: '42'
print(type(y)) # Output: <class 'str'>
```

## Converting List to Tuple

```
my_list = [1, 2, 3]
my_tuple = tuple(my_list) # Explicitly casting list to tuple
print(my_tuple) # Output: (1, 2, 3)
```

## Converting String to Float

```
num_str = "45.67"
num_float = float(num_str) # Explicitly casting string to
float
print(num_float) # Output: 45.67
```

## Using Boolean Casting

```
print(bool(0))    # Output: False (0 is considered False)
print(bool(1))    # Output: True
print(bool(""))   # Output: False (Empty string is considered
False)

print(bool("Hi"))  # Output: True (Non-empty string is
considered True)
```

### When to Use Casting

1. **Data Compatibility**: When passing variables to functions or operations that require a specific data type.

```
age = "25" # String
print("Next year, you'll be", int(age) + 1) # Convert string
to int
```

2. **Data Processing**: For example, reading data from user

input or files (often as strings) that needs to be converted for calculations.

```
num1 = input("Enter a number: ") # Always returns a
string
num2 = input("Enter another number: ")
result = int(num1) + int(num2) # Convert strings to
integers
print("Sum:", result)
```

3. **Precision**: To control the type of output in operations involving floats and integers.

## Key Notes

- Use casting cautiously to avoid errors. For instance, converting a non-numeric string to an integer will raise a ValueError.
- print(int("hello"))  # Raises ValueError: invalid literal for int()
- Python's implicit casting is automatic and safe, but explicit casting gives more control.

By understanding and using casting effectively, you can write flexible and robust Python programs.

# CHAPTER 03: CONDITIONAL STATEMENTS (IF, ELIF, ELSE)

Welcome to another exciting chapter in our journey through Python! Today, we'll explore one of the most powerful tools in programming: conditional statements. These statements allow you to control the flow of your program based on certain conditions—helping your code make decisions. We'll break down the key concepts with plenty of examples to make sure you understand how and when to use them. By the end of this chapter, you'll be making decisions in your code like a pro.

## What Are Conditional Statements?

Conditional statements are the building blocks for making decisions in Python. They enable your program to choose between different paths based on certain conditions, like "Is the user's input valid?" or "Should I keep running this loop?"

The primary conditional statements in Python are:

- **if**: This statement checks whether a condition is True and executes a block of code if it is.
- **elif** (else if): If the if condition is False, the elif statement checks another condition and executes its block of code if true.
- **else**: If none of the if or elif conditions are True, the else block will execute.

**Syntax of Conditional Statements**

Let's quickly review the basic syntax:

```
if condition:
    # code block to execute if condition is true
elif another_condition:
    # code block to execute if the second condition is true
else:
    # code block to execute if none of the conditions are true
```

**Example 1: Simple if Statement**

Let's start with the most basic form of a conditional statement. In this example, we'll check if a number is greater than 10.

```
number = 12

if number > 10:
    print("The number is greater than 10!")
```

**Explanation**: The program checks if number is greater than 10. Since 12 is greater than 10, it prints the message.

**Example 2: if and else Statement**

What if the number isn't greater than 10? We can use the else block to handle the other case.

```
number = 8

if number > 10:
    print("The number is greater than 10!")
else:
```

```
print("The number is less than or equal to 10.")
```

**Explanation**: Since 8 is not greater than 10, the else block will be executed, printing the alternative message.

## Example 3: Using elif for Multiple Conditions

You can use the elif statement when you want to check multiple conditions. In this case, let's check if the number is positive, negative, or zero.

```
number = -3

if number > 0:
    print("The number is positive.")
elif number < 0:
    print("The number is negative.")
else:
    print("The number is zero.")
```

**Explanation**: The program checks if the number is greater than zero. If not, it checks if it's less than zero. If neither condition is true, the else block is executed, indicating the number is zero.

## Example 4: Nested Conditional Statements

Sometimes, you might need to make decisions within decisions. This is where **nested conditional statements** come in. In this example, we'll check the age of a person and categorize them into different age groups.

```
age = 25

if age >= 18:
    if age < 40:
        print("You are an adult.")
    else:
        print("You are middle-aged.")
else:
    print("You are a minor.")
```

**Explanation**: The program first checks if the person is at least 18 years old. If they are, it checks whether they are under 40 to categorize them as an adult or middle-aged. If they are under 18, the program labels them as a minor.

## Example 5: Combining Multiple Conditions With And And Or

Python allows you to combine conditions with logical operators like and and or. This is useful when you want to check multiple conditions at once. Let's see how we can check if a number is within a certain range.

```
number = 15

if number > 10 and number < 20:
    print("The number is between 10 and 20.")
else:
    print("The number is outside the range.")
```

**Explanation**: The program checks if the number is both greater than 10 **and** less than 20. If both conditions are true, it prints the message; otherwise, it prints the alternative message.

### Tips and Tricks for Conditional Statements

- **Short-circuiting with and and or**: In Python, the logical and and or operators have short-circuit behaviour, meaning the second condition won't even be checked if the first condition already determines the result.
  - Example: If the first condition in an and statement is False, the second one is never evaluated.
- **Indentation matters**: Python relies on indentation to define blocks of code. Ensure your if, elif, and else blocks are properly indented to avoid errors.

### A Fun Challenge for You!

Now that you understand the basic conditional statements, let's try something fun. Write a program that asks for a user's age and determines if they are eligible for a senior citizen discount (age 65+), a student discount (age 18-25), or no discount. Make sure to handle all possibilities using if, elif, and else.

Here's a hint to get you started:

```
age = int(input("Please enter your age: "))

# Write Your code in editor!
```

## Summary

Conditional statements allow you to create flexible programs that can adapt to different situations based on the input they receive or conditions they encounter. With if, elif, and else, you can handle various scenarios and make your code responsive and dynamic.

We've covered several ways to use conditional statements, including:

- Basic if checks.
- else for alternative actions.
- elif to handle multiple conditions.
- Nested conditionals for complex decision-making.
- Combining conditions with and and or.

*In the next chapter, we'll dive deeper into loops and how to use them in conjunction with conditionals for even more dynamic behaviour. But for now, keep practicing and experimenting with what you've learned!*

# CHAPTER 04: FOR AND WHILE LOOPS IN PYTHON

**W**elcome to a new chapter of Python! Today, we're going to unlock the power of loops. Loops allow us to repeat tasks and handle repetitive actions efficiently—saving us from writing the same code over and over again. There are two primary types of loops in Python: the for loop and the while loop. Let's break down how each one works and how you can use them effectively in your programs.

## *What Are Loops and Why Do We Use Them?*

Loops are essential in programming for automating repetitive tasks. Imagine you need to print 100 numbers, perform an operation on each item in a list, or even process a file line by line. Instead of writing the same code 100 times, loops allow you to do this automatically. This makes your code cleaner, more efficient, and easier to maintain.

In Python, we have two types of loops:

- **for loop**: Used when you know how many times you

want to repeat a block of code (or when you are iterating over a sequence like a list, string, or range).

- **while loop**: Used when you want the loop to continue as long as a condition is true (the number of iterations might not be known upfront).

## The For Loop: Iterating Over Sequences

The for loop is used to iterate over a sequence of elements, such as a list, string, or a range of numbers. It's useful when you know in advance how many times you want to loop through something.

**Syntax of a for loop:**

```
for item in sequence:
    # code to execute for each item
```

Here's a simple example that prints out each element in a list:

```
fruits = ["apple", "banana", "cherry"]
for fruit in fruits:
    print(fruit)
```

**Explanation**: The loop goes through each item in the fruits list and prints it.

### Example 1: Looping Through a Range of Numbers

One of the most common uses of the for loop is to iterate over a range of numbers using the range() function. The range() function generates a sequence of numbers.

```
for number in range(1, 6):
    print(number)
```

**Explanation**: This will print the numbers 1 through 5. The range() function starts at 1 and goes up to (but does not include) 6.

## Example 2: Iterating Over a String

You can also use a for loop to iterate through each character in a string.

```
word = "hello"
for letter in word:
    print(letter)
```

**Explanation**: The loop will print each letter in the string "hello" one by one.

## Example 3: Using the for Loop with a List of Numbers

The for loop is often used to perform operations on each element in a list. Here's an example where we square each number in a list.

```
numbers = [1, 2, 3, 4, 5]
for number in numbers:
    print(number ** 2)
```

**Explanation**: This will print the square of each number in the list, outputting 1, 4, 9, 16, 25.

## Example 4: Using for with else

The else block after a for loop runs only if the loop completes without hitting a break statement. Here's an example where we search for a number in a list:

```
numbers = [2, 4, 6, 8, 10]
search = 5

for number in numbers:
    if number == search:
        print(f"Found {search}!")
        break
else:
    print(f"{search} not found.")
```

**Explanation**: The loop checks if 5 is in the list. If it finds it, it breaks out of the loop and prints that it was found. If the loop finishes without finding the number, the else block executes.

## The While Loop: Repeating Until A Condition Is False

The while loop runs as long as a condition remains True. Unlike the for loop, where the number of iterations is typically known beforehand, the while loop will keep going until the condition you specify becomes False.

### Syntax of a while loop:

```
while condition:
    # code to execute while condition is true
```

### Example 5: Basic while Loop

Here's an example of a simple while loop that prints numbers from 1 to 5:

```
count = 1
while count <= 5:
    print(count)
    count += 1
```

**Explanation**: The loop will keep running as long as count is less than or equal to 5. After each iteration, count is incremented by 1.

### Exercise 1: Print the First 10 Numbers in the Fibonacci Sequence

The Fibonacci sequence is a series of numbers where each number is the sum of the two preceding ones, starting from 0 and 1. Let's write a program that prints the first 10 numbers in the Fibonacci sequence.

```
a, b = 0, 1
count = 0
```

```
while count < 10:
    print(a)
    a, b = b, a + b
    count += 1
```

**Explanation**: This program uses a while loop to print the first 10 Fibonacci numbers. It initializes two variables a and b to represent the first two numbers in the sequence. Then, it updates a and b in each iteration.

## Nested Loops: Loops Inside Loops

Sometimes, you need to repeat a loop within another loop. These are called nested loops. They are useful when you need to handle multidimensional structures (like matrices) or create complex patterns.

### Example 6: Creating a Multiplication Table Using Nested Loops

A common example of a nested loop is generating a multiplication table. Let's create one from 1 to 10.

```
for i in range(1, 11):
    for j in range(1, 11):
        print(f"{i} * {j} = {i * j}")
```

**Explanation**: This nested for loop iterates over numbers from 1 to 10 and prints the result of multiplying i and j.

### Exercise 2: Create a Multiplication Table Using Nested Loops

Now, it's your turn to challenge yourself! Write a program that prints a multiplication table for numbers from 1 to 5, but in a formatted way where each row is neatly aligned.

## Creating Patterns With Loops

Loops are great for creating patterns! With just a few lines of code, you can generate shapes, pyramids, and other interesting structures using loops.

### Example 7: Printing a Pyramid Pattern of Stars

Here's a fun example of how you can create a pyramid pattern using a for loop:

```
height = 5

for i in range(1, height + 1):
    print(" " * (height - i) + "*" * (2 * i - 1))
```

**Explanation**: This loop generates a pyramid pattern of stars. For each row, it prints spaces followed by stars, with the number of stars increasing as we go down the pyramid.

### Exercise 3: Write a Program That Prints a Pyramid Pattern of Stars

Now, let's challenge you! Try writing a program that prints a pyramid pattern with the number of stars being user-defined. The user should input how many rows the pyramid will have.

### Summary

In this chapter, we've explored:

1. **for loops**: These are perfect for iterating over sequences and ranges. We learned how to use for loops to loop through lists, ranges, and even strings.
2. **while loops**: Great for repeating actions as long as a condition holds true. We saw how to use a while loop for tasks like printing Fibonacci numbers.
3. **Nested loops**: Loops inside loops help you handle more complex tasks, such as generating multiplication

tables.

4. **Creating patterns**: Loops allow you to generate beautiful shapes, like pyramids, stars, and other patterns.

---

*Loops are a fundamental concept in programming, and mastering them will make your code more efficient and your programming journey a lot more fun! Keep experimenting with different patterns and try solving challenges on your own.*

In the next chapter, we will dive deeper into functions and explore how to create reusable code blocks that make your programs even more powerful!

---

# CHAPTER 5: FUNCTIONS AND REUSABILITY

W elcome to another exciting chapter! Today, we're diving into one of the most important concepts in Python programming functions. Functions are the building blocks of clean, efficient, and reusable code. They allow us to group a set of instructions together and reuse them without repeating ourselves. In this chapter, we'll cover the basics of functions, how to define and call them, and how to work with parameters, arguments, and return values.

Let's explore how functions can make our code simpler, more organized, and scalable!

## What Are Functions?

A **function** is a block of code that only runs when it is called. Functions allow you to avoid repeating the same code over and over again. You define a function once and call it whenever needed, passing different values (known as arguments) to get different results.

Think of a function as a machine. You input some data (called arguments), the machine does some work, and then it spits out a result (called a return value).

## Why Do We Use Functions?

- **Reusability**: Once you write a function, you can call it as many times as you need without rewriting the code.
- **Simplicity**: Functions help break down complex problems into smaller, manageable parts.
- **Organization**: They help keep your code organized and easier to read.

### Syntax of Functions

Here's the basic syntax for defining a function in Python:

```
def function_name(parameters):
    # code block
    return result
```

- **def**: This keyword is used to define a function.
- **function_name**: The name of the function. It should be descriptive of what the function does.
- **parameters**: These are the values you pass into the function when calling it.
- **return**: This keyword sends the result back to the caller.

### Example 1: A Simple Function

Let's start with a simple example. We will write a function that prints a greeting message.

```
def greet(name):
    print(f"Hello, {name}!")
```

```
greet("Alice")
greet("Bob")
```

**Explanation**: The greet function takes one parameter name and prints a greeting message. We call the functon twice, once with the argument "Alice" and once with "Bob". The function runs each time we call it.

## Exercise 1: Write a Function that Converts Temperatures Between Celsius and Fahrenheit

Let's write a function that converts temperatures from Celsius to Fahrenheit and vice versa.

Here's the formula for conversion:

- Celsius to Fahrenheit: F = C * 9/5 + 32
- Fahrenheit to Celsius: C = (F - 32) * 5/9

```
def convert_temperature(value, scale):
    if scale == "C":
        return value * 9 / 5 + 32  # Convert Celsius to
Fahrenheit
    elif scale == "F":
        return (value - 32) * 5 / 9  # Convert Fahrenheit to
Celsius
    else:
        return "Invalid scale! Please use 'C' for Celsius or 'F'
for Fahrenheit."

print(convert_temperature(25, "C"))  # Convert 25°C to
Fahrenheit
print(convert_temperature(77, "F"))  # Convert 77°F to
Celsius
```

**Explanation**: This function accepts two arguments: value (the temperature) and scale (either "C" for Celsius or "F" for Fahrenheit). Depending on the scale, it performs the corresponding conversion and returns the result.

# Writing And Calling Functions

Once we've defined a function, we can call it whenever we need it in our program. Calling a function involves specifying its name and providing any necessary arguments.

Let's explore how to write and call more complex functions, using multiple functions in a program.

## Example 2: Calculating Area and Perimeter of a Rectangle

We will write two functions: one for calculating the **area** and another for calculating the **perimeter** of a rectangle. Then we will call both functions in a program.

```
def calculate_area(length, width):
    return length * width

def calculate_perimeter(length, width):
    return 2 * (length + width)

# Calling the functions
length = 5
width = 3
area = calculate_area(length, width)
perimeter = calculate_perimeter(length, width)

print(f"The area of the rectangle is: {area}")
print(f"The perimeter of the rectangle is: {perimeter}")
```

**Explanation**: The calculate_area function computes the area by multiplying the length and width. The calculate_perimeter function computes the perimeter by adding the length and width and multiplying the result by 2. We call both functions to calculate and print the area and perimeter.

## Exercise 2: Build a Program that Uses Multiple Functions to Calculate the Area and Perimeter of a Rectangle

Now it's your turn! Write a program where the user inputs the length and width of a rectangle. Use functions to calculate the area and perimeter, and print the results.

## Arguments, Parameters, And Return Values

In Python, functions can take **parameters** and return **values**. Parameters are the inputs to the function, and the return value is the output.

- **Parameters**: These are the variables you pass to the function when calling it. They allow you to work with different data inside your function.
- **Arguments**: These are the actual values that are passed into the function when it is called.
- **Return values**: A function can return a value that can be used later in the program.

Let's break this down with an example.

### Example 3: Function That Returns the Average of a List of Numbers

We will write a function that takes a list of numbers, calculates their average, and returns the result.

```python
def calculate_average(numbers):
    total = sum(numbers)
    average = total / len(numbers)
    return average

numbers = [10, 20, 30, 40, 50]
average = calculate_average(numbers)
print(f"The average of the list is: {average}")
```

**Explanation**: The calculate_average function takes a list of numbers, calculates the sum using the sum() function, and then divides it by the length of the list to find the average. The function returns the average, and we print it.

**Exercise 3: Create a Function that Takes a List of Numbers and Returns Their Average**

Now it's your turn to implement a similar program. Write a function that takes a list of numbers entered by the user and returns the average.

## Fun Exercises To Create Reusable Code

The true power of functions lies in their **reusability**. Once a function is written, you can reuse it across different programs. Let's design some fun and useful functions that you can reuse!

**Example 4: Generating a Random Password**

Let's write a function that generates a random password of a specified length. The password will contain a mix of uppercase and lowercase letters, numbers, and special characters.

```python
import random
import string

def generate_password(length):
    characters = string.ascii_letters + string.digits + string.punctuation
    password = ''.join(random.choice(characters) for _ in range(length))
    return password

# Generate a random password of length 12
password = generate_password(12)
print(f"Your random password is: {password}")
```

**Explanation**: The generate_password function uses the random module to randomly select characters from a pool of uppercase and lowercase letters, digits, and punctuation. It then creates a password of the specified length.

**Exercise 4: Design a Function that Generates a Random Password**

Create a function that lets the user specify the length of the password and returns a randomly generated password based on that length.

## Lambda Function In Python

A **lambda function** is a small, anonymous function in Python that can have any number of arguments but only one expression. Unlike regular functions defined using def, a lambda function is written in a single line.

**Syntax:**

lambda arguments: expression

- **arguments**: Input parameters for the lambda function.
- **expression**: A single expression evaluated and returned.

Lambda functions are often used when a function is required temporarily, especially as an argument to higher-order functions like map(), filter(), or sorted().

**Example 1: A Simple Lambda Function**

The following example demonstrates a lambda function to calculate the square of a number.

```
# Regular function
def square(x):
    return x ** 2

# Lambda function equivalent
```

```
square_lambda = lambda x: x ** 2

# Using the lambda function
print(square_lambda(5)) # Output: 25
```

In this example:

- The lambda function lambda x: x ** 2 takes one argument x and returns its square.
- It achieves the same result as the regular square function but in a concise form.

### Example 2: Using Lambda in map()

The map() function applies a lambda function to each item in an iterable (e.g., list).

```
# List of numbers
numbers = [1, 2, 3, 4, 5]

# Using a lambda function to double each number
doubled = list(map(lambda x: x * 2, numbers))

print(doubled) # Output: [2, 4, 6, 8, 10]
```

In this example:

- lambda x: x * 2 doubles each element in the numbers list.
- map() applies the lambda function to every element, and the result is converted to a list.

### Example 3: Using Lambda in sorted()

You can use a lambda function as a key in the sorted() function to customize the sorting order.

```
# List of tuples
data = [(1, 'apple'), (3, 'banana'), (2, 'cherry')]

# Sort by the second item in each tuple (the string)
sorted_data = sorted(data, key=lambda x: x[1])
```

```
print(sorted_data)
# Output: [(1, 'apple'), (3, 'banana'), (2, 'cherry')]
```

In this example:

- lambda x: x[1] extracts the second element of each tuple for sorting.
- The sorted() function uses this to sort the list by the string values.

## When to Use Lambda Functions

- When a small function is needed temporarily.
- For simple operations where defining a full function with def is unnecessary.
- As arguments to higher-order functions (map(), filter(), sorted(), etc.).

## Limitations of Lambda Functions

- They are limited to a single expression (no multi-line logic).
- Lack readability for complex operations compared to regular functions.

## Key Takeaways

- Lambda functions are concise and often used for short-lived, simple operations.
- They are especially useful in functional programming contexts (e.g., map, filter).
- Use them sparingly for readability, especially for complex logic.

## Summary

In this chapter, we've covered the following key concepts:

1. **What are functions?**: Functions are blocks of code that

perform specific tasks and can be reused throughout your program.

2. **Writing and calling functions**: We saw how to define functions, pass arguments, and call them to perform specific tasks.

3. **Arguments, parameters, and return values**: Functions can accept parameters (inputs) and return values (outputs). This makes them flexible and reusable.

4. **Fun exercises for reusability**: We created reusable functions for converting temperatures, calculating the area and perimeter of a rectangle, finding averages, and generating random passwords.

---

*By now, you should have a good understanding of how to write reusable code with functions. The more you practice using functions, the better you'll get at organizing and structuring your programs. In the next chapter, we'll explore another important concept working with modules and how to structure large projects. Happy coding!*

# CHAPTER 6: DATA STRUCTURES

W elcome to one of the most practical chapters in Python programming: Data Structures. Data structures are tools to store, organize, and manipulate data efficiently. In Python, data structures are incredibly versatile and simple to use. This chapter will cover the most common ones lists, tuples, dictionaries, and sets and discuss when and why you should use each.

By the end of this chapter, you'll be comfortable using these data structures to solve real-world problems. Let's dive in!

## Lists, Tuples, And Dictionaries

## Lists

- **Lists**

- A **list** in Python is an ordered and mutable collection

of items. Lists are used to store multiple items in a single variable. A list is defined using square brackets [] and the items are separated by commas( , ).

**Why Use Lists?**
- **Ordered** : Items are stored in the order you add them.
- **Dynamic** : You can add, remove, or modify elements.
- **Versatile** : Lists can hold any data type.

- Lists can contain items of any data type: integers, strings, floats, other lists, etc.
- Lists allow **duplicate values**.
- Lists are **mutable**, meaning you can change their content after creation.

Lists are one of the most versatile and commonly used data structures in Python.

**Example of a List:**

```
# Creating a simple list
my_list = ["apple", "banana", "cherry"]
print(my_list)
# Output: ['apple', 'banana', 'cherry']
```

## 1) Create Lists

You can create lists in various ways:

**a) Using Square Brackets []:**

```
# Creating a list
fruits = ["apple", "banana", "cherry"]
print(fruits)
# Output: ['apple', 'banana', 'cherry']
```

**b) Using the list() Constructor:**

```
# Using list() function
numbers = list((1, 2, 3, 4))
print(numbers)
# Output: [1, 2, 3, 4]
```

## c) Creating an Empty List:

```
# Empty list
empty_list = []
print(empty_list)
# Output: []
```

## 2) Access Items in Lists

You can access list items using their **index**. List indices start at 0.

### a) Access by Index:

```
fruits = ["apple", "banana", "cherry"]
print(fruits[0]) # Accessing the first item
# Output: apple
```

### b) Access Using Negative Index:

```
print(fruits[-1]) # Accessing the last item
# Output: cherry
```

### c) Access a Range of Items:

```
print(fruits[0:2]) # Accessing a range (index 0 to 1)
# Output: ['apple', 'banana']
```

## 3) Change Items in Lists

You can change the value of a specific item by referring to its index.

```
# Change an item
fruits = ["apple", "banana", "cherry"]
fruits[1] = "blueberry" # Replacing 'banana'
print(fruits)
# Output: ['apple', 'blueberry', 'cherry']
```

## 4) Add Items in Lists

You can add items to a list using various methods:

### a) Using append() Method:

```
# Append a single item
fruits = ["apple", "banana"]
fruits.append("cherry")
print(fruits)
# Output: ['apple', 'banana', 'cherry']
```

### b) Using insert() Method:

```
# Insert at a specific index
fruits.insert(1, "blueberry")
print(fruits)
# Output: ['apple', 'blueberry', 'banana', 'cherry']
```

### c) Using extend() Method:

```
# Add multiple items
fruits.extend(["mango", "grapes"])
print(fruits)
# Output: ['apple', 'blueberry', 'banana', 'cherry', 'mango', 'grapes']
```

### 5) Remove Items in Lists

You can remove items from a list using several methods:

### a) Using remove() Method:

```
# Remove a specific item
fruits = ["apple", "banana", "cherry"]
fruits.remove("banana")
print(fruits)
# Output: ['apple', 'cherry']
```

### b) Using pop() Method:

```
# Remove item by index
```

```
fruits.pop(1)  # Removes the item at index 1
print(fruits)
# Output: ['apple', 'cherry']
```

### c) Using del Keyword:

```
# Delete an item
fruits = ["apple", "banana", "cherry"]
del fruits[0]  # Deletes the first item
print(fruits)
# Output: ['banana', 'cherry']
```

### d) Using clear() Method:

```
# Clear all items from the list
fruits.clear()
print(fruits)
# Output: []
```

## 6) Loop Through Lists

You can loop through a list to access its items.

### a) Using for Loop:

```
fruits = ["apple", "banana", "cherry"]
for fruit in fruits:
    print(fruit)
# Output:
# apple
# banana
# cherry
```

### b) Loop Using Index:

```
for i in range(len(fruits)):
    print(fruits[i])
# Output:
# apple
```

```
# banana
# cherry
```

## 7) Copy Lists

You can copy lists using:

### a) copy() Method:

```
fruits = ["apple", "banana"]
copy_fruits = fruits.copy()
print(copy_fruits)
# Output: ['apple', 'banana']
```

### b) list() Constructor:

```
copy_fruits = list(fruits)
print(copy_fruits)
# Output: ['apple', 'banana']
```

## 8) Nested Lists

A list can contain other lists (nested structure):

```
matrix = [
    [1, 2, 3],
    [4, 5, 6],
    [7, 8, 9]
]
print(matrix[1][1]) # Accessing element at row 1, column 1
# Output: 5
```

## 9) List Methods

Here are some useful methods for lists:

| Method | Description |
|---|---|
| append() | Adds an item to the end of the list |

| clear() | Removes all items from the list |
|---|---|
| copy() | Returns a copy of the list |
| count() | Returns the count of a specific item |
| extend() | Adds all items from another iterable |
| index() | Returns the index of the first matching item |
| insert() | Inserts an item at a specified index |
| pop() | Removes an item by index |
| remove() | Removes the first occurrence of an item |
| reverse() | Reverses the list in place |
| sort() | Sorts the list (ascending by default) |

**Example:**

```
fruits = ["cherry", "apple", "banana"]
fruits.sort()
print(fruits)
# Output: ['apple', 'banana', 'cherry']
```

**10) Lists Exercises**

Test your knowledge with these exercises:

1. **Create** a list of five favourite fruits.
2. **Access** the third item in the list.
3. **Add** a new fruit to the list using append().
4. **Insert** a fruit at the second position in the list.
5. **Remove** the last item from the list using pop().
6. **Loop** through the list and print all items.
7. **Copy** the list into another variable.
8. Create a **nested list** to represent a 3x3 matrix.

By mastering lists, you'll gain a fundamental understanding of Python's versatile data structures for managing sequences of data!

# Tuples

A tuple is like a list but **immutable** (cannot be changed after creation). Tuples are ideal for storing data that should not be modified.

## Why Use Tuples?

- **Immutable**: Safer for storing constant data.
- **Faster**: Operations on tuples are generally faster than on lists due to their immutability.

## Syntax:

```
# Creating a tuple
my_tuple = (1, 2, 3)
```

## Example 1: Accessing Tuple Elements

```
coordinates = (10.5, 25.3)
print(coordinates[0])   # Output: 10.5
```

## Example 2: Tuple Packing and Unpacking

```
person = ("Alice", 30, "Engineer")
name, age, profession = person   # Unpacking
print(f"Name: {name}, Age: {age}, Profession: {profession}")
```

## Example 3: Tuples in Functions

```
def get_dimensions():
    return (1920, 1080)
width, height = get_dimensions()
print(f"Width: {width}, Height: {height}")
```

## Example 4: Nested Tuples

```
data = ((1, 2), (3, 4), (5, 6))
print(data[1][1])   # Output: 4
```

**Example 5: Tuple Methods**

Tuples come with the following methods:

- **count(x)**: Returns the number of occurrences of element x in the tuple.

Example:

```
t = (1, 2, 3, 2, 1)
print(t.count(2))   # Output: 2
```

- **index(x)**: Returns the index of the first occurrence of element x. If x is not found, it raises a ValueError.

Example:

```
t = (1, 2, 3, 2, 1)
print(t.index(3))   # Output: 2
```

# What Can You Do With Tuples?

Here's a section for your Python book covering the listed points with examples:

**Working with Tuples**

1. **Access elements using indexing, just like lists**

   You can access individual elements of a tuple using indexing, similar to lists. Tuples are zero-indexed, so the first element is at index 0.

Example:

```
my_tuple = (10, 20, 30, 40, 50)
print(my_tuple[0])   # Output: 10
print(my_tuple[3])   # Output: 40
```

2. **Slice tuples to get sub-tuples**

   Just like lists, you can slice a tuple to get a sub-tuple. The syntax for slicing is [start:end], where start is inclusive, and end is exclusive.

Example:

```
my_tuple = (10, 20, 30, 40, 50)
sub_tuple = my_tuple[1:4]
print(sub_tuple)   # Output: (20, 30, 40)
```

3. **Concatenate tuples using the + operator**

   You can concatenate two or more tuples using the + operator, creating a new tuple with the combined elements.

Example:

```
tuple1 = (1, 2, 3)
tuple2 = (4, 5, 6)
combined_tuple = tuple1 + tuple2
print(combined_tuple)   # Output: (1, 2, 3, 4, 5, 6)
```

4. **Repeat tuples using the * operator**

   You can repeat the elements of a tuple by using the * operator. This will create a new tuple with the repeated values.

Example:

```
my_tuple = (1, 2, 3)
repeated_tuple = my_tuple * 3
print(repeated_tuple)   # Output: (1, 2, 3, 1, 2, 3, 1, 2, 3)
```

5. **Use tuple methods like count() and index() to analyze the data**

   - count(x): Returns the number of occurrences of element x in the tuple.
   - index(x): Returns the index of the first occurrence of element x. Raises ValueError if x is not found.

Example:

```
my_tuple = (1, 2, 3, 2, 1)
print(my_tuple.count(2))   # Output: 2
print(my_tuple.index(3))   # Output: 2
```

6. **Store multiple values in a single tuple, including mixed data types**

Tuples can store different types of data, such as integers, floats, strings, and more.

Example:

```
mixed_tuple = (1, 3.14, "hello", True)
print(mixed_tuple)  # Output: (1, 3.14, 'hello',
True)
```

7. **Use tuples as keys in dictionaries, as they are hashable and immutable**

Since tuples are immutable, they can be used as keys in dictionaries, unlike lists.

Example:

```
my_dict = { (1, 2): "A", (3, 4): "B" }
print(my_dict[(1, 2)])  # Output: A
```

8. **Return multiple values from a function as a tuple**

Tuples are often used to return multiple values from a function. You can return a tuple directly from the function.

Example:

```
def get_user_info():
    return ("Alice", 30, "Engineer")

user_info = get_user_info()
print(user_info)  # Output: ('Alice', 30, 'Engineer')
```

9. **Nested tuples can be used for complex data structures, such as matrices or coordinate systems**

Tuples can also be nested inside other tuples, making them useful for representing complex data structures like matrices or coordinate systems.

Example:

```
matrix = ((1, 2), (3, 4), (5, 6))
```

```
print(matrix[1][0])   # Output: 3 (Second row, first
element)

coordinates = ((1, 2), (3, 4), (5, 6))
print(coordinates[2])   # Output: (5, 6)
```

# Dictionaries

A **dictionary** in Python is an unordered collection of key-value pairs. It is one of the most important and flexible data types in Python. A dictionary is defined using curly braces {} and consists of keys and values separated by a colon ( : ).

- Keys must be **unique** and **immutable** (e.g., strings, numbers, or tuples).
- Values can be of **any type** (e.g., strings, lists, other dictionaries, etc.).

Dictionaries are highly efficient for data lookups because they use a hashing mechanism to map keys to values.

**Example of a Dictionary:**

```
# Creating a simple dictionary
my_dict = {
    "name": "John",
    "age": 30,
    "city": "New York"
}
print(my_dict)
# Output: {'name': 'John', 'age': 30, 'city': 'New York'}
```

## 1) Create Dictionaries

You can create dictionaries in various ways:

### a) Using Curly Braces {}:

```
# Creating a dictionary
```

```python
person = {
    "name": "Alice",
    "age": 25,
    "job": "Engineer"
}
print(person)
# Output: {'name': 'Alice', 'age': 25, 'job': 'Engineer'}
```

### b) Using the dict() Constructor:

```python
# Using dict() function
car = dict(brand="Toyota", model="Corolla", year=2020)
print(car)
# Output: {'brand': 'Toyota', 'model': 'Corolla', 'year': 2020}
```

### c) Creating an Empty Dictionary:

```python
# Empty dictionary
empty_dict = {}
print(empty_dict)
# Output: {}
```

## 2) Access Items in Dictionaries

You can access dictionary values using keys.

### a) Access Using Key:

```python
person = {
    "name": "Alice",
    "age": 25,
    "city": "London"
}
print(person["name"]) # Accessing 'name' key
# Output: Alice
```

### b) Using get() Method:

```python
print(person.get("age")) # Safer way to access a key
# Output: 25
```

### c) Access Non-Existent Key:

```
    print(person.get("salary", "Not Found")) # Returns default
    value if key is missing
    # Output: Not Found

        print(person.get("salary", "Not Found")) # Returns
    default value if key is missing
        # Output: Not Found
```

## 3) Change Items in Dictionaries

You can change the value of a specific key.

```
# Change a value
person = {
    "name": "Alice",
    "age": 25
}
person["age"] = 26
print(person)
# Output: {'name': 'Alice', 'age': 26}
```

## 4) Add Items in Dictionaries

You can add new key-value pairs to a dictionary.

```
# Adding new key-value pair
person = {
    "name": "Alice"
}
person["city"] = "Paris"
print(person)
# Output: {'name': 'Alice', 'city': 'Paris'}
```

## 5) Remove Items in Dictionaries

You can remove items using various methods:

### a)  Using pop() Method:

```
    person = {
```

```
    "name": "Alice",
    "age": 25
}
person.pop("age")  # Removes the 'age' key
print(person)
# Output: {'name': 'Alice'}
```

### b) Using del Keyword:

```
del person["name"]  # Deletes the 'name' key
print(person)
# Output: {}
```

### c) Using popitem() Method:

```
# Removes the last inserted item
car = {   "brand": "Ford", "year": 2022}
car.popitem()
print(car)
# Output: {'brand': 'Ford'}
```

### d) Using clear() Method:

```
car.clear()  # Clears all items
print(car)
# Output: {}
```

## 6) Loop Through Dictionaries

You can loop through keys, values, or key-value pairs:

### a) Loop Through Keys:

```
person = {   "name": "Alice",  "age": 25}
for key in person:
    print(key)
# Output:
# name
# age
```

### b) Loop Through Values:

```
for value in person.values():
    print(value)
# Output:
# Alice
# 25
```

### c) Loop Through Key-Value Pairs:

```
for key, value in person.items():
    print(key, value)
# Output:
# name Alice
# age 25
```

## 7) Copy Dictionaries

You can copy dictionaries using:

### a) copy() Method:

```
original = {"name": "Alice", "age": 25}
copy_dict = original.copy()
print(copy_dict)
# Output: {'name': 'Alice', 'age': 25}
```

### b) dict() Constructor:

```
copy_dict = dict(original)
print(copy_dict)
# Output: {'name': 'Alice', 'age': 25}
```

## 8) Nested Dictionaries

A dictionary can contain other dictionaries (nested structure):

```
family = {
    "child1": {"name": "Anna", "age": 5},
    "child2": {"name": "Tom", "age": 7}
}
```

```
print(family["child1"]["name"]) # Accessing nested
dictionary
# Output: Anna
```

## 9) Dictionary Methods

Here are some useful methods for dictionaries:

| Method | Description |
|---|---|
| clear() | Removes all items from the dictionary |
| copy() | Returns a copy of the dictionary |
| get() | Returns the value for a given key |
| items() | Returns a view of key-value pairs |
| keys() | Returns a view of dictionary keys |
| pop(key) | Removes the item with the specified key |
| popitem() | Removes the last inserted key-value pair |
| setdefault() | Inserts a key with a default value |
| update() | Updates the dictionary with another dict |
| values() | Returns a view of dictionary values |

**Example:**

```
person = {"name": "Alice", "age": 25}
person.update({"city": "Paris"})
print(person)
```

**# Output: {'name': 'Alice', 'age': 25, 'city': 'Paris'}**

## 10) Dictionaries Exercises

Test your knowledge with these exercises:

1. **Create** a dictionary to store a student's details: name, age, and grade.
2. **Access** the grade of the student from the dictionary.
3. **Add** a new key-value pair for the student's school name.
4. **Update** the student's grade.
5. **Remove** the age of the student using the pop() method.
6. **Loop** through the dictionary to print all key-value pairs.
7. **Copy** the dictionary into another variable.
8. Create a **nested dictionary** to store details of two students.

---

By mastering dictionaries, you'll have a powerful tool to store and manipulate structured data in Python!

**Exercise**: Write a Program to store and display information about your favourite books

Create a program using dictionaries to store book titles, authors, and ratings. Display this information in a readable format.

---

## Sets And Their Uses

A   set   is an unordered collection of unique elements. It's great for removing duplicates and performing mathematical operations like unions and intersections.

### Why Use Sets?

- **Unique elements**: Automatically removes duplicates.
- **Fast operations**: Efficient for membership tests and set operations.

### Syntax:

```
#Creating a set
my_set = {1, 2, 3, 3}   Duplicate 3 will be removed
```

### Example 1: Removing Duplicates

```
numbers = [1, 2, 2, 3, 4, 4, 5]
unique_numbers = set(numbers)
print(unique_numbers)  {1, 2, 3, 4, 5}
```

### Example 2: Membership Testing

```
my_set = {"apple", "banana", "cherry"}
print("banana" in my_set)   True
```

### Example 3: Set Operations

```
A = {1, 2, 3}
B = {3, 4, 5}
print(A | B)   Union: {1, 2, 3, 4, 5}
print(A & B)   Intersection: {3}
print(A - B)   Difference: {1, 2}
```

### Example 4: Adding and Removing Elements

```
fruits = {"apple", "banana"}
fruits.add("cherry")   Adding
fruits.remove("banana")   Removing
print(fruits)
```

### Example 5: Frozen Sets

```
frozen = frozenset([1, 2, 3])   Immutable set
print(frozen)
```

**Exercise**: Create a Program That Finds Unique Elements in a List

Write a program that accepts a list of numbers and outputs only the unique elements using a set.

**When and Why to Use Each Data Structure**

| Data Structure | Use Case |
|---|---|
| List | When you need an ordered, mutable collection. |
| Tuple | For immutable collections (e.g., coordinates). |
| Dictionary | For key-value mappings (e.g., user profiles). |
| Set | For unique elements and set operations. |

## Hands-On Projects With Data Structures

### Example 1: Contact Book Program

Let's create a program that stores names, phone numbers, and emails using a dictionary.

```
contacts = {}

  #Adding a contact
def add_contact(name, phone, email):
    contacts[name] = {"phone": phone, "email": email}
```

```
#Displaying all contacts
```

```
def display_contacts():
    for name, info in contacts.items():
        print(f"Name: {name}, Phone: {info['phone']}, Email: {info['email']}")
```

```
# Example usage
add_contact("Alice", "123-456-7890", "alice@example.com")
add_contact("Bob", "987-654-3210", "bob@example.com")
display_contacts()
search_contact("Alice")
search_contact("Charlie")
```

# CHAPTER 7: WORKING WITH FILES IN PYTHON

One of the most powerful features of Python is its ability to work with files. Files allow you to save data, read information, and share it between programs. This chapter will guide you through reading from and writing to files, working with CSV and text files, and understanding JSON for modern data storage.

## Reading From And Writing To Files

Python makes it easy to handle files using built-in functions. The `open()` function is your gateway to working with files.

### Syntax:

```
#Open a file
file = open("filename", "mode")
```

**The modes are:**

- **r** : Read (default)
- **w** : Write (overwrites the file if it exists)
- **a** : Append (adds content to the end of the file)
- **r+**: Read and Write

### Example 1: Writing to a File

```
with open("example.txt", "w") as file:
    file.write("Hello, world!\n")
    file.write("This is a new file.")
print("File written successfully.")
```

### Example 2: Reading from a File

```
with open("example.txt", "r") as file:
    content = file.read()
    print(content)
```

### Example 3: Reading a File Line by Line

```
with open("example.txt", "r") as file:
    for line in file:
        print(line.strip())
```

### Example 4: Appending to a File

```
with open("example.txt", "a") as file:
    file.write("\nAppending new content!")
```

### Example 5: Checking if a File Exists

```
import os
if os.path.exists("example.txt"):
    print("File exists!")
else:
```

```
    print("File does not exist.")
```

**Exercise:**
Write a program that reads a text file and counts the
number of words.

## Working With Csv And Text Files

CSV (Comma-Separated Values) files are a common way to store
structured data, like spreadsheets or simple databases.

### Example 1: Writing to a CSV File

```
import csv
with open("data.csv", "w", newline="") as csvfile:
    writer = csv.writer(csvfile)
    writer.writerow(["Name", "Age", "City"])
    writer.writerow(["Alice", 25, "New York"])
    writer.writerow(["Bob", 30, "Los Angeles"])
```

### Example 2: Reading a CSV File

```
import csv
with open("data.csv", "r") as csvfile:
    reader = csv.reader(csvfile)
    for row in reader:
        print(row)
```

### Example 3: Using Dictionaries with CSV

```
import csv
with open("data.csv", "w", newline="") as csvfile:
    fieldnames = ["Name", "Age", "City"]
    writer = csv.DictWriter(csvfile, fieldnames=fieldnames)
    writer.writeheader()
    writer.writerow({"Name": "Alice", "Age": 25, "City": "New
York"})
    writer.writerow({"Name": "Bob", "Age": 30, "City": "Los
Angeles"})
```

### Example 4: Reading CSV into Dictionaries

```
import csv
with open("data.csv", "r") as csvfile:
    reader = csv.DictReader(csvfile)
    for row in reader:
        print(row)
```

### Example 5: Handling Large CSV Files

```
import csv
with open("large_data.csv", "r") as csvfile:
    reader = csv.reader(csvfile)
    for i, row in enumerate(reader):
        if i > 10:   Read only the first 10 rows
            break
        print(row)
```

**Exercise:**
Create a program that writes and reads user data to/from a CSV file.

## Introduction To Json

JSON (JavaScript Object Notation) is a lightweight data format that is easy to read and write. It is commonly used for APIs and data exchange.

### Syntax:

A JSON object looks like a Python dictionary:

```
{
    "name": "Alice",
    "age": 25,
    "is_student": false
}
```

In Python, JSON data is handled using the `json` module.

### Example 1: Writing JSON Data to a File

```
import json
data = {
    "name": "Alice",
    "age": 25,
    "is_student": False
}
with open("data.json", "w") as jsonfile:
    json.dump(data, jsonfile)
```

### Example 2: Reading JSON Data from a File

```
import json
with open("data.json", "r") as jsonfile:
    data = json.load(jsonfile)
    print(data)
```

**Example 3: Working with Nested JSON**

```python
import json
data = {
    "user": {
        "name": "Alice",
        "details": {
            "age": 25,
            "city": "New York"    }  }}
with open("nested_data.json", "w") as jsonfile:
    json.dump(data, jsonfile)
with open("nested_data.json", "r") as jsonfile:
    data = json.load(jsonfile)
    print(data["user"]["details"]["city"])   New York
```

**Example 4: Converting JSON to a Python Object**

```python
import json
json_string = '{"name": "Alice", "age": 25}'
data = json.loads(json_string)
print(data["name"])   Alice
```

**Example 5: Converting a Python Object to JSON**

```python
import json
person = {
    "name": "Bob",
    "age": 30,
    "skills": ["Python", "Java"] }
json_string = json.dumps(person, indent=4)
print(json_string)
```

> **Exercise:**
> Build a program that saves and loads user preferences using JSON.

With these concepts in hand, you now have the tools to work with files, CSVs, and JSON data effectively. Try the exercises and experiment to gain confidence!

# CHAPTER 8: ERROR HANDLING AND DEBUGGING

E rrors are inevitable in programming. Even experienced developers encounter bugs and exceptions. This chapter will help you understand common Python errors, how to handle them gracefully, and how to debug your code efficiently. By mastering error handling and debugging, you'll save time and create more reliable programs.

## Common Python Errors And How To Fix Them

### Types of Errors:

1. **Syntax Errors**: Mistakes in the code structure.

   **Example**: Missing a colon or parentheses.

2. **Runtime Errors**: Occur during code execution.

   **Example**: Dividing by zero or accessing a non-existent file.

3. **Logical Errors**: Code runs but produces incorrect results.

   **Example**: Misplaced conditions in an `if` statement.

## Example 1: Fixing a Syntax Error

```
# Incorrect Code
if True
    print("Hello")

# Corrected Code
if True:
    print("Hello")
```

## Example 2: Handling Division by Zero

```
# Incorrect Code
result = 10 / 0

# Fixed Code
try:
    result = 10 / 0
except ZeroDivisionError:
    print("Cannot divide by zero!")
```

## Example 3: Correcting a Logical Error

```
# Incorrect Code
x = 5
if x > 10:
    print("x is less than 10")

# Fixed Code
x = 5
if x < 10:
    print("x is less than 10")
```

### Example 4: File Not Found Error

```python
# Incorrect Code
with open("nonexistent_file.txt", "r") as file:
    content = file.read()

# Fixed Code
try:
    with open("nonexistent_file.txt", "r") as file:
        content = file.read()
except FileNotFoundError:
    print("The file does not exist.")
```

### Example 5: Index Out of Range

```python
# Incorrect Code
numbers = [1, 2, 3]
print(numbers[5])

# Fixed Code
numbers = [1, 2, 3]
if len(numbers) > 5:
    print(numbers[5])
else:
    print("Index out of range.")
```

**Exercise:** Identify and Fix Errors in a Buggy Script

**Given the following buggy code, fix all the errors:**

```python
# Buggy Code
def greet(name)
print("Hello, " + name)
greet(123)
```

## Using 'try', 'except', and 'finally'

*Python's 'try', 'except' block is used to handle exceptions, while `finally` ensures clean-up operations are performed.*

Syntax:

```
try:
    # Code that may raise an exception
except ExceptionType:
    # Handle the exception
finally:
    # Code that runs no matter what
```

### Example 1: Handling Multiple Exceptions

```
try:
    x = int(input("Enter a number: "))
    y = 10 / x
except ValueError:
    print("Please enter a valid number.")
except ZeroDivisionError:
    print("Cannot divide by zero.")
```

### Example 2: Using `finally`

```
try:
    file = open("example.txt", "r")
    content = file.read()
except FileNotFoundError:
```

```
    print("File not found.")
finally:
    print("Execution completed.")
```

## Example 3: Custom Exception Handling

```python
class NegativeNumberError(Exception):
    pass
def check_positive(number):
    if number < 0:
        raise NegativeNumberError("Number cannot be
negative.")
try:
    check_positive(-5)
except NegativeNumberError as e:
    print(e)
```

## Example 4: Nested Try-Except Blocks

```python
try:
    try:
        result = 10 / int(input("Enter a number: "))
    except ValueError:
        print("Invalid input.")
except ZeroDivisionError:
    print("Cannot divide by zero.")
```

## Example 5: Logging Exceptions

```python
import logging
try:
    result = 10 / 0
except ZeroDivisionError as e:
    logging.error(f"An error occurred: {e}")
```

> **Exercise**: Write a Program That Handles File-Not-Found Errors Gracefully

## Debugging Tips And Tools

Debugging is the art of finding and fixing issues in your code. Python provides several tools and techniques to make this process easier.

### Tip 1: Use Print Statements

Adding print statements can help you understand what your code is doing at each step.

### Example 1: Debugging with Print Statements

```python
def add_numbers(a, b):
    print(f"Adding {a} and {b}")
    return a + b
result = add_numbers(5, "10")
```

### Tip 2: Use Python Debugger (`pdb`)

The `pdb` module allows step-by-step debugging.

### Example 2: Debugging with `pdb`

```python
import pdb
def divide(a, b):
    pdb.set_trace()
    return a / b
result = divide(10, 0)
```

### Tip 3: Leverage IDE Debugging Tools

Most Python IDEs (like PyCharm or VSCode) have built-in debugging tools, allowing you to set breakpoints and inspect variables.

### Example 3: Debugging a Function

```python
def multiply(a, b):
    result = a * b
    return result
# Use an IDE to set a breakpoint on the line below
result = multiply(5, "2")
```

### Tip 4: Use Assertions

Assertions ensure your code meets certain conditions during execution.

### Example 4: Debugging with Assertions

```python
x = -10
assert x >= 0, "x must be non-negative"
```

### Tip 5: Use Logging

Logging helps track code execution without cluttering your output with print statements.

### Example 5: Adding Logging

```python
import logging
logging.basicConfig(level=logging.DEBUG)
def add(a, b):
    logging.debug(f"Adding {a} and {b}")
    return a + b
result = add(5, 10)
```

> **Exercise**: Debug a Provided Script Using Print Statements or a Debugger Tool

Given the following code, use debugging techniques to find and fix the errors:

```
# Debug this Code
def calculate_area(radius):
    return 3.14 * radius * radius
radius = "10"
print("Area:", calculate_area(radius))
```

# CHAPTER 9: PYTHON AND GAMES

P ython is not just about data processing and automation; it's also a fantastic tool for creating games! This chapter introduces you to the basics of game design, text-based adventures, and graphical games using libraries like Pygame. Let's explore how you can bring your creative ideas to life with Python.

## Basics Of Game Design With Python

Game design involves creating interactive experiences for users. Python provides a great starting point, even for beginners, with its simplicity and versatile libraries.

### Example 1: Guess the Number Game

```
import random
number_to_guess = random.randint(1, 100)
tries = 0
print("Welcome to the Guess the Number Game!")
while True:
    guess = int(input("Enter your guess (1-100): "))
```

```
    tries += 1
    if guess < number_to_guess:
        print("Too low! Try again.")
    elif guess > number_to_guess:
        print("Too high! Try again.")
    else:
        print(f"Congratulations! You guessed the number in
{tries} tries.")
        break
```

## Example 2: Rock-Paper-Scissors

```
import random
choices = ["rock", "paper", "scissors"]
computer_choice = random.choice(choices)
user_choice = input("Choose rock, paper, or scissors:
").lower()

if user_choice == computer_choice:
    print("It's a tie!")
elif (user_choice == "rock" and computer_choice ==
"scissors") or \
    (user_choice == "scissors" and computer_choice ==
"paper") or \
    (user_choice == "paper" and computer_choice == "rock"):
    print("You win!")
else:
    print("You lose! The computer chose", computer_choice)
```

## Example 3: Simple Dice Roller

```
import random
def roll_dice():
    return random.randint(1, 6)
print("Rolling the dice...")
```

```
print("You rolled a:", roll_dice())
```

## Example 4: Number Guessing with Difficulty Levels

```python
import random
def set_difficulty():
    level = input("Choose difficulty (easy, medium, hard): ").lower()
    if level == "easy":
        return 10
    elif level == "medium":
        return 7
    else:
        return 5
number_to_guess = random.randint(1, 50)
attempts = set_difficulty()
print("Guess the number between 1 and 50")
while attempts > 0:
    guess = int(input("Your guess: "))
    attempts -= 1

    if guess == number_to_guess:
        print("Congratulations! You guessed the number.")
        break
    elif guess < number_to_guess:
        print("Too low!", end=" ")
    else:
        print("Too high!", end=" ")

    print(f"Attempts left: {attempts}")

if attempts == 0:
    print("Game over! The number was", number_to_guess)
```

### Example 5: Word Scramble Game

```
import random
def scramble(word):
    scrambled = list(word)
    random.shuffle(scrambled)
    return ''.join(scrambled)
word_list = ["python", "coding", "developer", "program"]
word_to_guess = random.choice(word_list)
scrambled_word = scramble(word_to_guess)
print("Unscramble this word:", scrambled_word)
guess = input("Your guess: ")
if guess == word_to_guess:
    print("Correct!")
else:
    print("Better luck next time! The word was",
word_to_guess)
```

### Exercise: Create a Basic "Guess the Number" Game
Design a game where the user has to guess a random number generated by the computer. Add feedback for each guess (e.g., "too high" or "too low") and allow the user to choose the difficulty level.

## Building A Text-Based Adventure Game

Text-based games are a fantastic way to dive into storytelling and interactivity. Let's create a simple adventure game where players make choices to progress.

### Example 1: Basic Adventure Structure

```
def start_game():
```

```
    print("Welcome to the Adventure Game!")
    print("You are standing in front of a dark forest.")
    choice = input("Do you want to ENTER the forest or RUN
away? ").lower()
    if choice == "enter":
        print("You bravely enter the forest...")
        explore_forest()
    else:
        print("You run away. Game over.")
def explore_forest():
    print("You encounter a wild animal!")
    action = input("Do you FIGHT or RUN? ").lower()
    if action == "fight":
        print("You defeated the animal. You win!")
    else:
        print("The animal caught you. Game over.")
start_game()
```

## Example 2: Treasure Hunt Game

```
def start_treasure_hunt():
    print("Welcome to the Treasure Hunt!")
    print("You have three doors in front of you: Red, Blue, and
Green.")
    choice = input("Which door do you choose? ").lower()
    if choice == "red":
        print("You found a room full of gold! You win!")
    elif choice == "blue":
        print("You fell into a trap. Game over.")
    elif choice == "green":
        print("You encountered a friendly wizard who gives
you a map to more treasures. You win!")
    else:
        print("Invalid choice. Game over.")
```

```
start_treasure_hunt()
` ` `
```

## Example 3: Multi-Level Choices

```python
def start_quest():
    print("Your mission is to rescue the princess.")
    choice = input("Do you take the LONG or SHORT path? ").lower()

    if choice == "long":
        print("You find a magical sword on the way.")
        final_battle(True)
    else:
        print("You reach the castle quickly but are unarmed.")
        final_battle(False)

def final_battle(has_weapon):
    print("You face the dragon!")
    if has_weapon:
        print("With the magical sword, you slay the dragon and rescue the princess. You win!")
    else:
        print("You have no weapon. The dragon defeats you. Game over.")

start_quest()
```

### Example 4: Inventory System

```python
inventory = []
def pick_item(item):
    inventory.append(item)
    print(f"You picked up a {item}.")

def show_inventory():
    print("Your inventory:", inventory)
```

```
print("You find a stick on the ground.")
pick_item("stick")

print("You find a shiny key.")
pick_item("key")

show_inventory()
```

### Example 5: Save and Load Progress

```
import json

game_state = {
    "location": "forest",
    "health": 100,
    "inventory": ["map", "torch"]
}

def save_game(state, filename="savegame.json"):
    with open(filename, "w") as file:
        json.dump(state, file)

save_game(game_state)
print("Game saved.")

with open("savegame.json", "r") as file:
    loaded_state = json.load(file)
    print("Game loaded:", loaded_state)
```

**Exercise**: Develop a Text-Based Treasure Hunt Game with Multiple Choices
Design a game where the player navigates through multiple choices to find hidden treasure. Incorporate branching storylines and an inventory system.

# Introduction to Libraries
# Like Pygame

Pygame is a popular Python library for creating graphical games. It provides tools for handling graphics, sounds, and user input.

- **Installing Pygame**

To install Pygame, run:

```
pip install pygame
# Example 1: Creating a Pygame Window
import pygame
pygame.init()
screen = pygame.display.set_mode((800, 600))
pygame.display.set_caption("My First Game")
running = True
while running:
    for event in pygame.event.get():
        if event.type == pygame.QUIT:
            running = False
pygame.quit()
```

# Example 2: Drawing Shapes

```
import pygame
pygame.init()
screen = pygame.display.set_mode((800, 600))
pygame.display.set_caption("Drawing Shapes")
running = True
while running:
    for event in pygame.event.get():
        if event.type == pygame.QUIT:
```

```python
        running = False
    screen.fill((0, 0, 0))  # Clear the screen
    pygame.draw.rect(screen, (255, 0, 0), (100, 100, 200,
100))  # Draw a red rectangle
    pygame.draw.circle(screen, (0, 255, 0), (400, 300), 50)  #
Draw a green circle
    pygame.display.flip()
pygame.quit()
```

◆ ◆ ◆

# CHAPTER 10:
# VISUALIZING IDEAS
# WITH PYTHON

V isualization is a powerful way to understand and communicate data. Python offers excellent libraries like matplotlib and seaborn that make creating stunning graphs and charts easy. This chapter introduces these tools and shows how to use them effectively.

## Introduction to matplotlib and seaborn

### Why Visualizations Matter

Visualizations simplify complex data and make patterns easier to spot. Whether it's a simple bar chart or an intricate heatmap, visualizations make data storytelling impactful.

#### Getting Started with `matplotlib`

`matplotlib` is a versatile library for creating static, interactive, and animated visualizations.

## Example 1: Creating a Basic Line Graph

```python
import matplotlib.pyplot as plt
x = [1, 2, 3, 4, 5]
y = [2, 4, 6, 8, 10]
plt.plot(x, y)
plt.title("Simple Line Graph")
plt.xlabel("X-axis")
plt.ylabel("Y-axis")
plt.show()
```

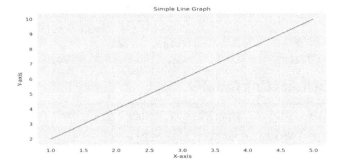

Picture 01: simple Line Graph

## Example 2: Creating a Bar Chart

```python
categories = ['Apples', 'Bananas', 'Cherries']
values = [5, 7, 3]
plt.bar(categories, values, color='skyblue')
plt.title("Fruit Count")
plt.show()
```

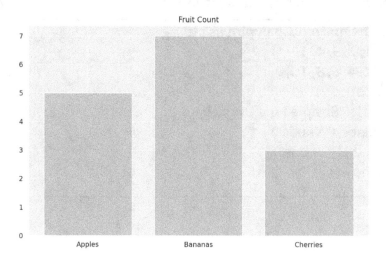

Picture 02: Bar Chart

### Example 3: Customizing Graphs

```
plt.plot(x, y, linestyle='--', marker='o', color='green')
plt.title("Customized Line Graph")
plt.grid()
plt.show()
```

## Enhancing Visualizations with `seaborn`

`seaborn` builds on `matplotlib`, offering higher-level functions and stunning themes.

### Example 4: Creating a Histogram

```
import seaborn as sns
import numpy as np
data = np.random.randn(1000)
sns.histplot(data, kde=True, color='purple')
plt.title("Distribution Plot")
plt.show()
```

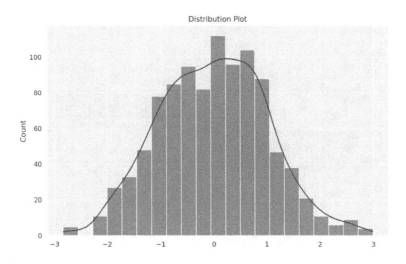

Picture 03: Histogram

## Example 5: Comparing Datasets with a Box Plot

```
import pandas as pd
  Sample data
data = pd.DataFrame({
    'Group A': np.random.randn(50),
    'Group B': np.random.randn(50) + 1 })
sns.boxplot(data=data)
plt.title("Box Plot Comparison")
plt.show()
```

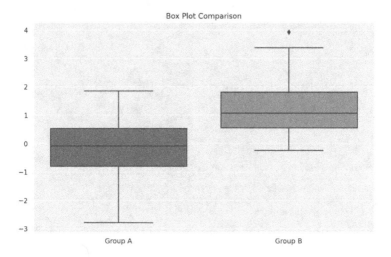

Picture 04: Box Plot

---

**Exercise: Create a Bar Chart and a Line Graph from a Dataset**

1. Load a dataset using `pandas`.
2. Create a bar chart to visualize category counts.
3. Use a line graph to observe trends over time.

---

# Creating Beautiful Graphs And Charts

Adding Style to Your Graphs

Seaborn themes like `darkgrid` and `whitegrid` make graphs visually appealing.

### Example 1: Applying Themes

```
sns.set_theme(style="darkgrid")
sns.lineplot(x=[1, 2, 3], y=[3, 5, 7], color="orange")
plt.title("Styled Line Plot")
plt.show()
```

# Visualizing Survey Results

## Example 2: Pie Chart

```
labels = ['Satisfied', 'Neutral', 'Unsatisfied']
sizes = [60, 25, 15]
colors = ['lightgreen', 'lightblue', 'salmon']
plt.pie(sizes, labels=labels, colors=colors, autopct='%1.1f%
%')
plt.title("Survey Results")
plt.show()
```

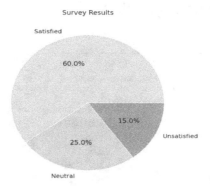

Picture 05: Pie Chart

## Example 3: Scatter Plot

```
sns.scatterplot(x=[1, 2, 3, 4], y=[4, 3, 2, 1], hue=['A', 'B', 'A', 'B'],
style=[0, 1, 0, 1])
plt.title("Scatter Plot Example")
plt.show()
```

# Advanced Techniques

## Example 4: Pair Plots

```
data = sns.load_dataset("iris")
sns.pairplot(data, hue="species")
plt.show()
```

## Example 5: Heatmaps

```
import numpy as np
data = np.random.rand(10, 10)
sns.heatmap(data, annot=True, cmap="coolwarm")
plt.title("Heatmap Example")
plt.show()
```

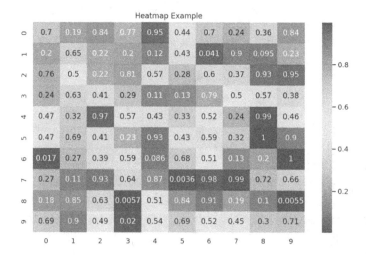

Picture 06: Heat Map

**Exercise: Visualize Survey Results Using Pie and Scatter Plots**

1. Create a pie chart for survey data showing different categories.

2. Create a scatter plot to analyze relationships between two variables.

# A Mini-Project: Visualizing Real-World Data

Objective: Build a Dashboard with Multiple Visualizations

In this mini-project, we'll use real-world data to create a simple dashboard.

Steps:

1. Choose a dataset, such as COVID-19 statistics, weather data, or financial trends.

2. Clean and pre-process the data.

3. Create the following visualizations:

- Line chart for trends.
- Bar chart for category-wise data.
- Pie chart for proportions.
- Heatmap for correlations.

### Example: Visualizing COVID-19 Data

```python
import pandas as pd
import seaborn as sns
import matplotlib.pyplot as plt
# Load the dataset
data = pd.read_csv("covid19_data.csv")

 #Line Chart
sns.lineplot(x="Date", y="Cases", data=data)
plt.title("COVID-19 Cases Over Time")
plt.show()

# Bar Chart
sns.barplot(x="Country", y="Cases", data=data)
plt.title("Cases by Country")
plt.show()

# Pie Chart
labels = data["Country"].unique()
sizes = data.groupby("Country")["Cases"].sum()
```

```
plt.pie(sizes, labels=labels, autopct='%1.1f%%')
plt.title("Cases Distribution")
plt.show()

# Heatmap
corr = data.corr()
sns.heatmap(corr, annot=True, cmap="coolwarm")
plt.title("Correlation Heatmap")
plt.show()
```

**Exercise: Use a Real-World Dataset to Create a Dashboard**

Find a dataset online (e.g., from Kaggle or public APIs).
Follow the steps to create a dashboard showcasing key
insights with visualizations.

By mastering these techniques, you can turn raw data into
stunning visuals that convey clear and impactful messages.

# CHAPTER 11: AUTOMATION MAGIC

H ave you ever wished a repetitive task could handle itself? With Python, it can! Automation is one of Python's most powerful capabilities, helping save time and eliminates human error. In this chapter, we'll explore how Python simplifies everyday tasks, from renaming files to scraping data from websites and even sending automated emails.

## Using Python To Automate Tasks

### Why Automate?

Repetitive tasks, such as file renaming or organizing folders, can be tedious. Automation not only saves time but also reduces the risk of manual errors. Python's libraries like `os` and `shutil` make this a breeze.

### Example 1: Renaming Multiple Files in a Directory

Suppose you have dozens of files with non-descriptive names, and you want to rename them in a structured way:

```
import os
```

```python
def rename_files(directory, prefix):
    for count, filename in enumerate(os.listdir(directory),
start=1):
        new_name = f"{prefix}_{count}
{os.path.splitext(filename)[1]}"
        os.rename(os.path.join(directory, filename),
os.path.join(directory, new_name))
  #Call the function
directory_path = "./files"
rename_files(directory_path, "Document")
print("Files renamed successfully!")
```

## Example 2: Copying and Organizing Files by Extension

```python
import os
import shutil
def organize_files(directory):
    for filename in os.listdir(directory):
        ext = os.path.splitext(filename)[1][1:]
        ext_folder = os.path.join(directory, ext.upper())
        os.makedirs(ext_folder, exist_ok=True)
        shutil.move(os.path.join(directory, filename),
os.path.join(ext_folder, filename))

organize_files("./downloads")
print("Files organized by type!")
```

## Example 3: Scheduling Python Scripts

You can schedule Python scripts to run at specific times using the `schedule` library:

```python
import schedule
import time
def task():
    print("Task executed!")
```

```
  #Schedule the task
schedule.every().day.at("10:00").do(task)
while True:
  schedule.run_pending()
  time.sleep(1)
```

### Exercise: Automate Renaming Multiple Files in a Directory

Write a script that renames image files in a folder, appending the date and a unique identifier to each file name.

## Web Scraping Basics With Beautiful Soup

### What is Web Scraping?

Web scraping is the process of extracting data from websites. Python's `BeautifulSoup` library makes it easy to navigate and parse HTML.

### Example 1: Extracting Article Titles and Links

```
from bs4 import BeautifulSoup
import requests
url = "https://example.com/news"
response = requests.get(url)
soup = BeautifulSoup(response.text, "html.parser")
articles = soup.find_all("article")
for article in articles:
    title = article.find("h2").text
    link = article.find("a")["href"]
    print(f"Title: {title}\nLink: {link}\n")
```

### Example 2: Scraping Weather Data

```
url = "https://example.com/weather"
```

```
response = requests.get(url)
soup = BeautifulSoup(response.text, "html.parser")

temperatures = [temp.text for temp in
soup.find_all(class_="temp")]
print("Today's temperatures:", temperatures)
```

**Example 3: Downloading Images from a Webpage**

```
import os
url = "https://example.com/gallery"
response = requests.get(url)
soup = BeautifulSoup(response.text, "html.parser")
images = soup.find_all("img")
for img in images:
    img_url = img["src"]
    img_data = requests.get(img_url).content
    with open(os.path.basename(img_url), "wb") as f:
        f.write(img_data)
print("Images downloaded!")
```

**Exercise: Scrape a Webpage to Extract Article Titles and Links**

Identify a news website and scrape the latest headlines, storing the results in a text file.

## Automating File Management And Emails

### Combining File Management and Email Automation

Python's `os`, `shutil`, and `smtplib` libraries can work together to automate file management tasks and send summaries via email.

### Example 1: Organizing Files by Type and Emailing a Summary

```python
import os
import shutil
import smtplib

  #File organization function
def organize_and_summarize(directory):
    summary = {}
    for filename in os.listdir(directory):
        ext = os.path.splitext(filename)[1][1:]
        ext_folder = os.path.join(directory, ext.upper())
        os.makedirs(ext_folder, exist_ok=True)
        shutil.move(os.path.join(directory, filename),
os.path.join(ext_folder, filename))
        summary[ext] = summary.get(ext, 0) + 1
    return summary

# Email function
def send_email(subject, body, to_email):
    smtp_server = "smtp.gmail.com"
    smtp_port = 587
    sender_email = "your_email@gmail.com"
    password = "your_password"

    with smtplib.SMTP(smtp_server, smtp_port) as server:
        server.starttls()
        server.login(sender_email, password)
        message = f"Subject: {subject}\n\n{body}"
        server.sendmail(sender_email, to_email, message)

# Organize and summarize
summary = organize_and_summarize("./downloads")
summary_text = "\n".join([f"{key}: {value} files" for key,
```

```
value in summary.items()])

  #Send email
send_email("File Organization Summary", summary_text,
"recipient@example.com")
print("Email sent successfully!")
```

## Example 2: Sending an Email with Attachments

```python
from email.mime.multipart import MIMEMultipart
from email.mime.text import MIMEText
from email.mime.base import MIMEBase
from email import encoders
import smtplib

  #Function to send email with attachment
def send_email_with_attachment(to_email, subject, body,
file_path):
    smtp_server = "smtp.gmail.com"
    smtp_port = 587
    sender_email = "your_email@gmail.com"
    password = "your_password"

    msg = MIMEMultipart()
    msg['From'] = sender_email
    msg['To'] = to_email
    msg['Subject'] = subject

    msg.attach(MIMEText(body, 'plain'))

    with open(file_path, "rb") as attachment:
        part = MIMEBase('application', 'octet-stream')
        part.set_payload(attachment.read())
        encoders.encode_base64(part)
        part.add_header('Content-Disposition', f'attachment;
filename={os.path.basename(file_path)}')
        msg.attach(part)
```

```
with smtplib.SMTP(smtp_server, smtp_port) as server:
    server.starttls()
    server.login(sender_email, password)
    server.send_message(msg)

send_email_with_attachment("recipient@example.com",
"Monthly Report", "Please find the report attached.",
"report.pdf")
print("Email with attachment sent!")
```

**Exercise**: Write a Program that Organizes Files by Type and Sends an Email with the Summary

Develop a script that organizes files in a folder, creates a summary report, and emails it to a recipient. Test it with a sample folder containing mixed file types.

Automation magic transforms tedious tasks into efficient workflows. With Python, you can turn hours of work into seconds. The possibilities are endless what will you automate next?

# CHAPTER 12:
# OBJECT-ORIENTED PROGRAMMING (OOP)

O bject-Oriented Programming (OOP) is a paradigm that structures code into reusable blueprints, called classes, which model real-world entities. This chapter explores OOP concepts and demonstrates how Python simplifies working with classes, objects, and related principles.

## *Understanding Classes and Objects*

### What Are Classes And Objects?

- Classes are blueprints for creating objects. They define attributes (data) and methods (functions).
- Objects are instances of classes, representing specific realizations of those blueprints.

**Let's start with a simple example:**

### Example 1: Defining and Using a Class

```python
class Dog:
    def __init__(self, name, breed):
        self.name = name
        self.breed = breed

    def bark(self):
        return f"{self.name} says Woof!"

 Creating an object
my_dog = Dog("Buddy", "Golden Retriever")
print(my_dog.bark())
```

### Example 2: Adding Attributes and Methods

```python
class Rectangle:
    def __init__(self, length, width):
        self.length = length
        self.width = width

    def area(self):
        return self.length  self.width

    def perimeter(self):
        return 2  (self.length + self.width)

rect = Rectangle(10, 5)
print("Area:", rect.area())
print("Perimeter:", rect.perimeter())
```

### Example 3: Modifying Object Attributes

```python
class Car:
    def __init__(self, make, model):
        self.make = make
```

```
        self.model = model

    def update_model(self, new_model):
        self.model = new_model

car = Car("Toyota", "Corolla")
car.update_model("Camry")
print(f"Updated Car Model: {car.model}")
```

## Example 4: Creating Multiple Objects

```
class Book:
    def __init__(self, title, author):
        self.title = title
        self.author = author

book1 = Book("1984", "George Orwell")
book2 = Book("Brave New World", "Aldous Huxley")
print(f"Book 1: {book1.title} by {book1.author}")
print(f"Book 2: {book2.title} by {book2.author}")
```

### Example 5: Adding Default Values

```
class Player:
    def __init__(self, name, level=1):
        self.name = name
        self.level = level

player = Player("Alice")
print(f"Player: {player.name}, Level: {player.level}")
```

### Exercise: Create a Bank Account Class
1. Define a class `BankAccount` with attributes for account holder and balance.
2. Add methods for depositing and withdrawing funds.
3. Create an object and test the methods.

*Inheritance, Polymorphism,*
*and Encapsulation*

## 1. Inheritance

Inheritance allows a class to inherit properties and methods from another class. It promotes code reuse and creates a hierarchical relationship between classes.

**Definition:**

Inheritance is the mechanism by which a new class (child class) can inherit attributes and methods from an existing class (parent class). This allows the child class to access or override the behaviour of the parent class.

**Explanation:**

- A **parent class** is the class whose properties and methods are inherited by another class.
- A **child class** inherits the attributes and methods of the parent class, allowing the child class to reuse and modify the functionality of the parent class.

**Example:**

```
# Parent class
class Animal:
    def speak(self):
        print("Animal makes a sound")

# Child class inherits from Animal
```

```
class Dog(Animal):
    def speak(self):
        print("Dog barks")

# Creating objects
animal = Animal()
dog = Dog()

# Accessing methods
animal.speak()   # Output: Animal makes a sound
dog.speak()      # Output: Dog barks
```

**Key Points:**

- The Dog class inherits the speak() method from the Animal class.
- The Dog class can override the inherited method to implement its own version of speak().

## 2. Polymorphism

Polymorphism means "many forms" and allows different classes to have methods with the same name but with different implementations. This enables objects of different classes to be treated as objects of a common superclass, but each having their own behavior for the method.

**Definition:**

Polymorphism allows the same method or function to behave differently depending on the object calling it. In Python, polymorphism can be achieved through method overriding (runtime polymorphism).

**Explanation:**

- **Method Overriding**: When a child class provides a specific implementation for a method that is already defined in the parent class.
- Polymorphism allows objects of different types to be

treated the same way but to respond in a type-specific manner.

**Example:**

```python
# Parent class
class Animal:
    def speak(self):
        print("Animal makes a sound")

# Child class 1
class Dog(Animal):
    def speak(self):
        print("Dog barks")

# Child class 2
class Cat(Animal):
    def speak(self):
        print("Cat meows")

# Function to demonstrate polymorphism
def animal_sound(animal):
    animal.speak()

# Creating objects
dog = Dog()
cat = Cat()

# Using polymorphism
animal_sound(dog)   # Output: Dog barks
animal_sound(cat)   # Output: Cat meows
```

**Key Points:**

- The animal_sound() function accepts any object that is an instance of the Animal class or its subclasses, but the behaviour of speak() depends on whether the object is of type Dog or Cat.
- This demonstrates **runtime polymorphism**.

# 3. Encapsulation

Encapsulation is the concept of bundling data and methods that operate on that data within a single unit, i.e., a class. It also restricts access to certain components of the object, which is known as **data hiding**.

**Definition:**

Encapsulation hides the internal state of an object and only exposes a controlled interface to interact with it. It is achieved by using access modifiers such as private, protected, and public.

**Explanation:**

- **Private attributes and methods** are those that are not accessible from outside the class. They are indicated by a leading underscore (_) or double underscore (__).
- **Public attributes and methods** are those that are accessible from outside the class.
- Encapsulation helps in protecting the integrity of an object by controlling the way the data is accessed or modified.

**Example:**

```
class BankAccount:
    def __init__(self, balance):
        self.__balance = balance  # Private attribute

    def deposit(self, amount):
        if amount > 0:
            self.__balance += amount

    def withdraw(self, amount):
        if amount > 0 and self.__balance >= amount:
            self.__balance -= amount

    def get_balance(self):
```

```
      return self.__balance  # Public method to access
private data

# Creating an object
account = BankAccount(1000)

# Using methods to interact with the private data
account.deposit(500)
account.withdraw(200)

# Accessing the private balance through a public method
print(account.get_balance())  # Output: 1300
```

## Key Points:

- The balance attribute is private and cannot be accessed directly from outside the class.
- The deposit() and withdraw() methods are public and provide a controlled way to modify the balance.
- The get_balance() method is a public method that allows access to the private balance attribute.

## 4. Attributes And Methods

**Definition:**

- **Attributes** are variables that store information about an object.
- **Methods** are functions defined inside a class that operate on its attributes.

**Explanation:**

- Attributes represent the data or state of an object.
- Methods define the behaviour or functionality of the object.

**Example:**

```
class Car:
    def __init__(self, brand, model):
        self.brand = brand  # Attribute
        self.model = model  # Attribute

    def display_info(self):
        print(f"This car is a {self.brand} {self.model}.")  #
Method

# Create an object
my_car = Car("Toyota", "Corolla")
my_car.display_info()
# Output: This car is a Toyota Corolla.
```

**Key Points:**

- Attributes are accessed using self inside the class.
- Methods operate on the attributes of the class.

---

## 5. Abstraction

**Definition:**
Abstraction is the process of hiding implementation details and exposing only the essential features of a class.

**Explanation:**

- Abstraction focuses on what an object does rather than how it does it.
- It is achieved using **abstract classes** and **abstract methods**.

**Example:**

```
from abc import ABC, abstractmethod

class Shape(ABC):
    @abstractmethod
    def area(self):
```

```
        pass

class Rectangle(Shape):
    def __init__(self, width, height):
        self.width = width
        self.height = height

    def area(self):
        return self.width * self.height

# Create an object
rectangle = Rectangle(5, 10)
print("Area of rectangle:", rectangle.area())
# Output: Area of rectangle: 50
```

## Key Points:

- An abstract class is defined using ABC (Abstract Base Class).
- Abstract methods must be implemented in the derived class.
- Abstraction allows us to define a template for classes and enforce method implementation.

---

By mastering lists and understanding concepts like attributes, methods, and abstraction, you'll have a solid foundation for programming in Python!

---

## Summary of Key OOP Principles:

1. **Inheritance**: Enables one class to inherit the properties and methods of another, promoting code reuse.

2. **Polymorphism**: Allows methods to have different implementations based on the object type, providing flexibility.

3. **Encapsulation**: Hides the internal data and ensures it can only be accessed or modified through controlled

interfaces, enhancing data security.

These principles help create more organized, modular, and maintainable code.

---

> **Exercise: Design a Class Hierarchy for Vehicles**
> 1. Create a parent class `Vehicle` with common attributes.
> 2. Create child classes `Car` and `Bike` that inherit from `Vehicle`.
> 3. Add unique methods to each class.

---

## Practical Examples Of Oop In Python

### Example 1: Library Management System

```python
class Book:
    def __init__(self, title, author):
        self.title = title
        self.author = author

class Library:
    def __init__(self):
        self.books = []

    def add_book(self, book):
        self.books.append(book)

    def display_books(self):
        for book in self.books:
            print(f"{book.title} by {book.author}")

lib = Library()
lib.add_book(Book("1984", "George Orwell"))
lib.add_book(Book("To Kill a Mockingbird", "Harper Lee"))
lib.display_books()
```

## Example 2: Employee Management System

```python
class Employee:
    def __init__(self, name, role):
        self.name = name
        self.role = role

class Company:
    def __init__(self):
        self.employees = []

    def hire(self, employee):
        self.employees.append(employee)

    def list_employees(self):
        for emp in self.employees:
            print(f"{emp.name}: {emp.role}")

company = Company()
company.hire(Employee("Alice", "Developer"))
company.hire(Employee("Bob", "Designer"))
company.list_employees()
```

## Example 3: Simple E-Commerce System

```python
class Product:
    def __init__(self, name, price):
        self.name = name
        self.price = price

class Cart:
    def __init__(self):
        self.products = []

    def add_product(self, product):
        self.products.append(product)
```

```
def checkout(self):
    total = sum([p.price for p in self.products])
    return f"Total: ${total}"

cart = Cart()
cart.add_product(Product("Laptop", 1200))
cart.add_product(Product("Mouse", 50))
print(cart.checkout())
```

**Exercise: Build a Library Management System**
1. Create a `Library` class to manage books.
2. Add functionality to lend, return, and display books.

*By mastering OOP, you unlock a powerful way to structure your Python code for clarity, reusability, and scalability.*

# CHAPTER 13: EXPLORING PYTHON LIBRARIES

P ython owes much of its versatility and power to its vast ecosystem of libraries. These libraries, ranging from data analysis to machine learning, allow you to perform complex tasks with just a few lines of code. This chapter introduces popular Python libraries, shows how to use them effectively, and walks you through small projects to solidify your learning.

## *Overview of Popular Python Libraries*

Python libraries provide pre-written code to perform specific tasks, saving you time and effort. Here are some of the most widely used libraries:

- **NumPy**: Numerical computing and array operations.
- **pandas**: Data manipulation and analysis.
- **matplotlib and seaborn** : Data visualization.
- **scikit-learn** : Machine learning.
- **Beautiful Soup**: Web scraping.

## Using Numpy For Array Operations

### Example 1: Creating Arrays

```python
import numpy as np
# Create a 1D array
array_1d = np.array([1, 2, 3, 4])
print("1D Array:", array_1d)

# Create a 2D array
array_2d = np.array([[1, 2], [3, 4]])
print("2D Array:\n", array_2d)
```

### Example 2: Array Arithmetic

```python
array = np.array([1, 2, 3])
print("Array + 1:", array + 1)
print("Array * 2:", array * 2)
```

### Example 3: Generating Arrays

```python
# Generate an array of zeros
zeros = np.zeros((2, 3))
print("Zeros Array:\n", zeros)

# Generate a range of numbers
range_array = np.arange(0, 10, 2)
print("Range Array:", range_array)
```

## Manipulating Dataframes With Pandas

### Example 4: Creating and Viewing DataFrames

```
import pandas as pd
data = {
    'Name': ['Alice', 'Bob', 'Charlie'],
    'Age': [25, 30, 35],
    'City': ['New York', 'Los Angeles', 'Chicago'] }
# Create a DataFrame
df = pd.DataFrame(data)
print(df)
```

### Example 5: DataFrame Operations

```
# Filtering rows
filtered_df = df[df['Age'] > 28]
print("Filtered DataFrame:\n", filtered_df)
# Adding a new column
df['Salary'] = [70000, 80000, 90000]
print("Updated DataFrame:\n", df)
```

**Exercise:** Perform Basic Operations on Arrays and DataFrames
1. Use NumPy to create a 3x3 matrix and calculate its transpose.
2. Create a pandas DataFrame to store student grades and calculate the average grade.

## When And How To Use Libraries Effectively

### Choosing the Right Library:

- Use NumPy for numerical tasks like matrix operations.
- Use pandas for data manipulation and cleaning.
- Use matplotlib or seaborn for data visualization.

**Best Practices:**

1. Read the documentation to understand the library's features.

2. Start with simple examples and gradually explore advanced functionality.

3. Combine libraries for more powerful solutions (e.g., pandas + matplotlib).

### Example 1: Cleaning Data with pandas

```
data = {
    'Name': ['Alice', 'Bob', 'Charlie', None],
    'Age': [25, None, 35, 40],
    'Salary': [70000, 80000, None, 50000]}
df = pd.DataFrame(data)
```

## Handling Missing Values

```
df.fillna({'Age': df['Age'].mean(), 'Salary': 0}, inplace=True)
print("Cleaned DataFrame:\n", df)
```

### Example 2: Combining NumPy and pandas

```
import numpy as np
import pandas as pd
array = np.random.randint(1, 100, size=(5, 3))
columns = ['Math', 'Science', 'English']
df = pd.DataFrame(array, columns=columns)
print("DataFrame from NumPy Array:\n", df)
```

### Example 3: Visualization with pandas and matplotlib

```python
import matplotlib.pyplot as plt

# Plotting a bar chart
df['Math'].plot(kind='bar', title='Math Scores')
plt.show()
```

**Exercise: Solve a Problem Using the pandas Library**
Create a pandas DataFrame with sales data for a store.
Calculate total sales, filter top-performing products, and
visualize the results.

## Building Small Projects With These Libraries

**Project:** Analyzing a Real-World Dataset

### 1. Load the Dataset

Example 1: Importing Data

```python
df = pd.read_csv("real_world_data.csv")
print("Data Preview:\n", df.head())
```

### 2. Clean and Process the Data

Example 2: Data Cleaning

```python
# Dropping rows with missing values
df.dropna(inplace=True)

# Converting a column to datetime
df['Date'] = pd.to_datetime(df['Date'])
```

### 3. Analyze the Data

Example 3: Statistical Analysis

Calculate summary statistics

```
print("Summary:\n", df.describe())
```

# 4. Visualize Insights

**Example 4:** Plotting Trends

```
import seaborn as sns
sns.lineplot(data=df, x='Date', y='Sales')
plt.title("Sales Over Time")
plt.show()
```

## 5. Automate Reporting

**Example 5:** Generating Reports

```
# Save analysis to a CSV file
summary = df.describe()
summary.to_csv("summary_report.csv")
```

---

**Exercise**: Build a Data Analysis Project Using a Real-World Dataset
1. Find a dataset online (e.g., weather, stock prices, or sports statistics).
2. Clean and preprocess the data.
3. Perform analysis and create visualizations.
4. Share your findings in a report.

---

By learning to use Python libraries effectively, you unlock the potential to tackle complex problems and build robust solutions with ease. Master these libraries to take your Python skills to the next level.

# CHAPTER 14: THE WORLD OF APIS

APIs (Application Programming Interfaces) allow different software systems to communicate with each other. They are like bridges, enabling your Python programs to interact with external services, fetch data, or even control devices. In this chapter, we will explore APIs, how to use them, and how to build a mini-project with an API.

## *What Are APIs and Why Are They Useful?*

- **Understanding APIs**

APIs define a set of rules that enable communication between applications. For example:

- A weather API provides weather data for any location.
- A stock market API gives access to real-time stock prices.
- A social media API lets you post content or retrieve user data programmatically.
- **Why Use APIs?**

**1. Access to External Data** : APIs allow you to fetch live data from services like Google Maps, Twitter, or Open Weather.

**2. Extend Functionality** : You can integrate features like payment processing or user authentication into your programs.

**3. Automation** : APIs make tasks like sending emails or managing cloud resources seamless.

### Example 1: API in Everyday Life

Imagine an online store that uses:

- A payment gateway API to handle transactions.
- A shipping API to track packages.
- A currency exchange API to display prices in multiple currencies.

> **Exercise:** Research and list three APIs you find interesting. Explore their documentation to see what data or features they offer.

## Accessing And Using Apis With Python

Python makes interacting with APIs easy using libraries like requests . Let's see how to fetch data from an API step by step.

### Example 2: Fetching Data from a Public API

This example fetches current weather data using the OpenWeatherMap API.

```
import requests
# Replace 'your_api_key' with an actual API key from
OpenWeatherMap
api_key = "your_api_key"
city = "New York"
url = f"http://api.openweathermap.org/data/2.5/weather?
```

```
q={city}&appid={api_key}&units=metric"

response = requests.get(url)
if response.status_code == 200:
    data = response.json()
    print(f"Weather in {city}:")
    print(f"Temperature: {data['main']['temp']} °C")
    print(f"Condition: {data['weather'][0]['description']}")
else:
    print("Failed to fetch weather data")
```

**Result:**

```
Weather in New York:
Temperature: 5 °C
Condition: clear sky
```

**Example 3:** Handling API Errors

```
response = requests.get("https://api.example.com/data")
if response.status_code == 200:
    print("Data fetched successfully!")
else:
    print(f"Error: {response.status_code}")
```

**Example 4:** Using Parameters in API Requests

Some APIs require parameters for specific queries. Let's fetch random jokes from the JokeAPI.

```
url = "https://v2.jokeapi.dev/joke/Programming"
params = {"type": "single"}  # Request a single-part joke
response = requests.get(url, params=params)
if response.status_code == 200:
    data = response.json()
    print("Joke:", data["joke"])
```

```
else:
    print("Failed to fetch joke")
```

Result:

```
Joke: Why do programmers prefer dark mode? Because light
attracts bugs!
```

### Example 5: Sending Data to an API

APIs can also accept data from your program. Here's how to send data to a mock API.

```
url = "https://jsonplaceholder.typicode.com/posts"
data = {
    "title": "Hello World",
    "body": "This is a test post",
    "userId": 1}
response = requests.post(url, json=data)
if response.status_code == 201:
    print("Post created successfully!", response.json())
else:
    print("Failed to create post")
```

**Result:**

```
Post created successfully! {'id': 101, 'title': 'Hello World',
'body': 'This is a test post', 'userId': 1}
```

# Building Your Own Mini Api-Based Project

## Project: Stock Price Analyzer

This project fetches stock prices using the Alpha Vantage API and analyzes the data.

1. Step 1: Setup and API Key

    - Sign up on Alpha Vantage and get a free API key.

2. Step 2: Fetch Stock Prices

```python
import requests
api_key = "your_api_key"
symbol = "AAPL"
url = f"https://www.alphavantage.co/query?
function=TIME_SERIES_DAILY&symbol={symbol}
&apikey={api_key}"
response = requests.get(url)
if response.status_code == 200:
    data = response.json()
    daily_data = data["Time Series (Daily)"]
    print("Latest Stock Prices:")
    for date, stats in list(daily_data.items())[:5]:
        print(f"Date: {date}, Close: {stats['4. close']}")
else:
    print("Failed to fetch stock data")
```

Result:

```
Latest Stock Prices:
Date: 2024-12-14, Close: 176.89
Date: 2024-12-13, Close: 178.45
```

3. **Step 3: Analyze Stock Performance**

```python
import matplotlib.pyplot as plt
# Extract closing prices
dates = list(daily_data.keys())[:10]
closing_prices = [float(daily_data[date]['4. close']) for date in dates]
```

```
# Plot the data
plt.plot(dates, closing_prices, marker='o')
plt.title("Stock Prices Over Time")
plt.xlabel("Date")
plt.ylabel("Closing Price")
plt.xticks(rotation=45)
plt.show()
```

**Result:**

A line graph displaying stock prices over time.

4. **Step 4: Add a Summary**

```
average_price = sum(closing_prices) / len(closing_prices)
print(f"Average Closing Price: ${average_price:.2f}")
```

**Result:**

Average Closing Price: $177.12

**Exercise: Build Your Own API-Based Project**
1. Choose an API (e.g., NASA, Spotify, or Google Maps).
2. Fetch and analyze data from the API.
3. Visualize the results with graphs or tables.

*APIs unlock a world of possibilities, allowing your Python programs to interact with powerful services and live data. Mastering APIs equips you to build dynamic, data-driven applications with ease.*

# CHAPTER 015
# PYTHON MODULES, MATH FUNCTIONS, AND DATE FUNCTIONS

## *Python Modules*

In Python, a module is a reusable collection of code that you can import and use in your programs. A module typically contains functions, classes, or variables that are logically related. It helps to organize code into manageable pieces and promotes reusability.

There are two main types of modules:

- **Built-in Modules**: These are pre-installed with Python, such as math, os, and datetime.
- **Custom Modules**: You can create your own modules by saving Python code in a .py file.

**How to Use a Module:**

To use the functionality of a module, you need to import it into your program using the import statement.

**Example:**

```
import math

# Using a function from the math module
square_root = math.sqrt(25)
print(f"The square root of 25 is: {square_root}")

#You can also import specific parts of a module:
from math import pi, factorial

print(f"The value of pi is: {pi}")
print(f"The factorial of 5 is: {factorial(5)}")
```

## Python Math Functions

The **math module** is a built-in Python library designed for advanced mathematical operations. It provides functions and constants that go beyond basic arithmetic, such as trigonometric calculations, logarithmic functions, and rounding operations.

**Popular Math Functions**:

- math.sqrt(x): Finds the square root of x.
- math.pow(x, y): Raises x to the power of y.
- math.ceil(x): Rounds x up to the nearest whole number.
- math.floor(x): Rounds x down to the nearest whole number.
- math.sin(x), math.cos(x), math.tan(x): Calculates the sine, cosine, and tangent of an angle in radians.
- math.log(x, base): Computes the logarithm of x with the specified base (default is the natural logarithm).

**Example:**

```
import math

# Working with constants and functions
circle_radius = 7
area = math.pi * math.pow(circle_radius, 2)
print(f"The area of a circle with radius 7 is: {area:.2f}")

# Trigonometric functions
angle_in_degrees = 90
angle_in_radians = math.radians(angle_in_degrees)

print(f"The sine of 90 degrees is:
{math.sin(angle_in_radians)}")
```

## Python Date Functions

The **datetime module** is Python's go-to library for working with dates and times. It offers tools to handle current dates, manipulate time intervals, and format date-time data in a human-readable way.

*Key Features:*

- datetime.datetime.now(): Fetches the current date and time.
- datetime.date(year, month, day): Creates a specific date object.

- datetime.datetime.strftime(format): Converts a date object into a formatted string.
- datetime.datetime.strptime(date_string,     format): Parses a formatted string into a date object.

**Example**:

```
import datetime

# Current date and time
current_time = datetime.datetime.now()
print(f"The current date and time is: {current_time}")

# Formatting dates
formatted_time = current_time.strftime("%A, %d %B %Y")
print(f"Today is: {formatted_time}")

# Parsing a string into a date
holiday = "2024-12-25"
holiday_date = datetime.datetime.strptime(holiday, "%Y-%m-%d")
print(f"The holiday is on: {holiday_date.strftime('%A, %B %d, %Y')}")
```

*By using modules like math and datetime, Python simplifies complex calculations and time handling, making it easier to write efficient and readable code.*

# CHAPTER 016
# MONGODB

## Introduction

MongoDB is a leading NoSQL database that breaks away from the constraints of traditional relational databases. It uses a document-oriented model to store data in JSON-like BSON (Binary JSON) format, making it highly scalable, flexible, and suitable for modern applications such as e-commerce platforms, content management systems, and real-time analytics tools.

**Definition**

MongoDB is an open-source, non-relational database designed to handle large amounts of data in a dynamic and flexible manner. Unlike relational databases with rigid schemas, MongoDB allows for dynamic schemas, making it an excellent choice for agile development environments.

**Real-time Example**

Imagine you're developing an online shopping platform. You need a database that can store product details, including their categories, pricing, specifications, and customer reviews, without enforcing a fixed structure. MongoDB's document model lets you do this effortlessly.

Here's an example of a product document in MongoDB:

```
{
  "_id": "prod123",
  "name": "Wireless Headphones",
  "price": 89.99,
  "category": "Electronics",
  "features": ["Bluetooth 5.0", "Noise Cancelling", "12-hour
Battery Life"],
  "reviews": [
    {"username": "user1", "rating": 5, "comment": "Excellent
sound quality!"},
    {"username": "user2", "rating": 4, "comment": "Good, but a
bit expensive."}
  ]
}
```

**Exercise**

1. Install MongoDB and create a database for a movie ticket booking system.

2. Create a sample collection to store movie details (e.g., title, duration, genre, and release date).

- **MongoDB Create Database**

In MongoDB, a database is created when you switch to it and start adding data. You don't need to explicitly create it beforehand. A database in MongoDB contains collections, which in turn store documents.

**Real-time Example**

Let's say you're building a school management system. You need a database to store details about students, teachers, and courses. To create a database named SchoolDB:

use SchoolDB

**Exercise**

- Create a database named LibraryDB.
- Add a collection named Books and insert sample book data.

---

- **MongoDB Collection**

A **collection** in MongoDB is analogous to a table in a relational database. It stores a group of related documents, but unlike a table, collections don't enforce a fixed schema.

**Real-time Example**

In a food delivery app, you might have a collection named Restaurants that stores information about various restaurants:

```
{
  "_id": "rest101",
  "name": "Spicy Villa",
  "cuisine": "Indian",
  "rating": 4.5,
  "menu": [
    {"dish": "Paneer Butter Masala", "price": 10.99},
    {"dish": "Garlic Naan", "price": 1.99}
  ]}
```

**Exercise**

1. Create a collection named Orders in a database named FoodDeliveryDB.
2. Insert sample orders with fields like customer name, items ordered, and delivery address.

---

- **MongoDB Insert**

The insert operation in MongoDB allows you to add documents to a collection. You can use insertOne() for a single document or insertMany() for multiple documents.

## Real-time Example

For an employee management system, you might add employee details to a collection named Employees:

```
# Insert one employee
db.Employees.insertOne({
  "name": "John Doe",
  "designation": "Software Engineer",
  "department": "IT",
  "salary": 75000 })

# Insert multiple employees
db.Employees.insertMany([
  {"name": "Jane Smith", "designation": "Manager",
"department": "HR", "salary": 85000},
  {"name": "Mike Brown", "designation": "Accountant",
"department": "Finance", "salary": 60000} ])
```

## Exercise

1.  Insert details of 5 products into a Products collection.
2.  Add data for 3 customers into a Customers collection.

---

- **MongoDB Find**

The find() method retrieves documents from a collection. You can filter results with queries or retrieve all documents.

## Real-time Example

In a library system, to find books by a specific author:

```
# Find all books by J.K. Rowling
db.Books.find({"author": "J.K. Rowling"})
```

## Exercise

1.  Find all students in a Students collection who scored above 90.
2.  Retrieve all orders placed in the last 7 days.

---

- **MongoDB Query**

Queries allow you to filter data based on specific conditions using operators like $gt (greater than), $lt (less than), $in (matches any value in an array), and more.

**Real-time Example**

In a retail app, find products priced between $20 and $50:

```
db.Products.find({"price": {"$gt": 20, "$lt": 50}})
```

**Exercise**

1. Write a query to find employees earning more than $50,000.

2. Query the Orders collection to find orders containing more than 3 items.

---

- **MongoDB Sort**

**Real-time Example**

To list products in ascending order of price:

```
db.Products.find().sort({"price": 1})
```

**Exercise**

1. Sort students by their grades in descending order.

2. Sort books by publication year in ascending order.

---

- **MongoDB Delete**

**Real-time Example**

Delete a product by its ID:

```
db.Products.deleteOne({"_id": "prod123"})
```

**Exercise**

1. Delete all inactive users from a Users collection.

2. Remove all books with a rating below 3.

---

- **MongoDB Drop Collection**

**Real-time Example**

Drop a collection:

```
db.tempData.drop()
```

**Exercise**

    1. Create and drop a collection named TemporaryData.

- **MongoDB Update**

**Real-time Example**

Update an employee's salary:

```
db.Employees.updateOne({"name": "John Doe"}, {"$set":
{"salary": 80000}})
```

**Exercise**

    1. Update the prices of all products in the Products collection by 10%.

- **MongoDB Limit**

**Real-time Example**

Fetch the first 5 documents:

```
db.Students.find().limit(5)
```

**Exercise**

    1. Retrieve the top 3 most expensive products.

    2. Limit the results to the first 10 orders.

# CHAPTER 017: PYTHON SQL MADE SIMPLE

## 1. Introduction To Mysql

**Description:**

MySQL is one of the most popular relational database management systems (RDBMS) that uses SQL (Structured Query Language) for interacting with data. Python provides libraries like mysql-connector-python and pymysql to connect and interact with MySQL databases seamlessly.

Example:

Installing the required library:

```
pip install mysql-connector-python
Connecting to a MySQL server:
import mysql.connector

# Establishing a connection
connection = mysql.connector.connect(
    host="localhost",
```

```
    user="your_username",
    password="your_password"
)
print("Connected to MySQL!")
```

**Exercise:**

- Install MySQL and set up a local server.
- Write a Python script to establish a connection with your MySQL server.

## 2. Creating A Database

**Description:**
Databases are containers for organizing and storing related data. In MySQL, databases are created using the CREATE DATABASE statement. Python can execute SQL commands via the cursor object.

Example:
Creating a database named School:

```
cursor = connection.cursor()
cursor.execute("CREATE DATABASE School")
print("Database 'School' created successfully!")
```

**Exercise:**

- Create a database named Library using Python.
- Check if the database exists by listing all databases.

### 3. Creating Tables
**Description:**
Tables are the core structure in a database where data is stored in rows and columns. Use the CREATE TABLE statement to define a table structure.

**Example:**
Creating a Students table in the School database:

```
cursor.execute("USE School")  # Switch to the 'School'
database
cursor.execute("""
CREATE TABLE Students (
    id INT AUTO_INCREMENT PRIMARY KEY,
    name VARCHAR(255),
    age INT,
    grade VARCHAR(10)
)""")
print("Table 'Students' created successfully!")
```

**Exercise:**

- Create a Books table in the Library database with fields for title, author, and year of publication.

## 4. Inserting Data into Tables

**Description:**

Data is added to tables using the INSERT INTO statement. Python allows parameterized queries to prevent SQL injection.

**Example:**

Inserting a record into the Students table:

```
query = "INSERT INTO Students (name, age, grade) VALUES
(%s, %s, %s)"
values = ("Alice", 14, "8th Grade")
cursor.execute(query, values)
connection.commit()
print(f"{cursor.rowcount} record inserted.")
```

**Exercise:**

- Insert 3 students into the Students table.
- Verify the data insertion by selecting all rows from the table.

## 5. Retrieving Data with SELECT

**Description:**

The SELECT statement retrieves data from tables. You can specify the columns to retrieve or use * to fetch all columns.

**Example:**

Retrieve all student records:

```
cursor.execute("SELECT * FROM Students")
for row in cursor.fetchall():
    print(row)
```

**Exercise:**

- Write a Python script to fetch and display only the names of all students.

## 6. Filtering Data with WHERE

**Description:**

The WHERE clause filters rows based on specified conditions. Use operators like =, >, <, and LIKE to refine queries.

**Example:**

Retrieve students older than 13:

```
cursor.execute("SELECT * FROM Students WHERE age > 13")
for row in cursor.fetchall():
    print(row)
```

**Exercise:**

- Find all students in the Students table with grades "A" or above.

## 7. Sorting Data with ORDER BY

**Description:**

The ORDER BY clause sorts query results in ascending (ASC) or descending (DESC) order.

**Example:**

Sort students by age in descending order:

```
cursor.execute("SELECT * FROM Students ORDER BY age
DESC")
```

```
for row in cursor.fetchall():
    print(row)
```

**Exercise:**

- Sort the Books table by publication year in ascending order.

### 8. Updating Records

**Description:**

The UPDATE statement modifies existing data in a table. Use the WHERE clause to specify which records to update.

**Example:**

Update the grade of a student named Alice:

```
cursor.execute("UPDATE Students SET grade = '9th Grade'
WHERE name = 'Alice'")
connection.commit()
print(f"{cursor.rowcount} record(s) updated.")
```

**Exercise:**

- Update all students' grades to "Promoted".

### 9. Deleting Records

**Description:**

The DELETE statement removes records from a table. Use the WHERE clause to prevent deleting all rows.

**Example:**

Delete a student with a specific ID:

```
cursor.execute("DELETE FROM Students WHERE id = 1")
connection.commit()
print(f"{cursor.rowcount} record(s) deleted.")
```

**Exercise:**

- Delete all books published before the year 2000 from the Books tab

## 10. Dropping Tables

**Description:**

The DROP TABLE statement removes a table and all its data from the database.

**Example:**

Drop the Students table:

```
cursor.execute("DROP TABLE Students")
print("Table 'Students' dropped successfully!")
```

**Exercise:**

- Create a temporary table and drop it using Python.

## 11. Limiting Query Results with LIMIT

**Description:**

The LIMIT clause restricts the number of rows returned by a query. This is useful for paginating results.

**Example:**

Retrieve the first 3 students:

```
cursor.execute("SELECT * FROM Students LIMIT 3")
for row in cursor.fetchall():
    print(row)
```

**Exercise:**

- Fetch the top 5 most recently added books from the Books table.

## 12. Joining Tables

**Description:**

Joins combine rows from multiple tables based on related columns. Types of joins include INNER JOIN, LEFT JOIN, and RIGHT JOIN.

**Example:**

Combine Students and Courses tables to list enrolled students:

```
query = """
SELECT Students.name, Courses.course_name
FROM Students
INNER JOIN Courses ON Students.id = Courses.student_id
"""
cursor.execute(query)
for row in cursor.fetchall():
    print(row)
```

**Exercise:**

- Create two tables (Authors and Books) and join them to display book titles along with author names.

# CHAPTER 018
# PYTHON DESKTOP
# SOFTWARE
# DEVELOPMENT
# FRAMEWORKS

## *1. Tkinter*

- **Description:**
  Tkinter is Python's standard GUI toolkit, bundled with Python by default. It's simple to use and suitable for small-to-medium desktop applications.
- **Features:**
  - Basic widgets like buttons, labels, and text boxes.
  - Support for custom dialogs and events.
- **Best For:** Beginners and lightweight applications.
- **Example:**

```python
import tkinter as tk

def say_hello():
    label.config(text="Hello, World!")

root = tk.Tk()
```

```
root.title("Tkinter Example")

label = tk.Label(root, text="Click the button!")
label.pack()

button = tk.Button(root, text="Click Me",
command=say_hello)
button.pack()

root.mainloop()
```

## 2. PyQt / PySide (Qt Framework)

- **Description:**
  PyQt and PySide are Python bindings for the Qt application framework, which provides powerful tools for building modern, feature-rich desktop apps.

- **Features:**
    - Advanced widgets and support for custom UIs.
    - Cross-platform support.
    - Designer tools for visual UI design.

- **Best For:** Professional-grade applications.

- **Example:**

```
from PyQt5.QtWidgets import QApplication, QLabel

app = QApplication([])
label = QLabel('Hello, PyQt!')
label.show()
app.exec_()
```

## 3. Kivy

- **Description:**
  Kivy is a modern library for developing multi-touch applications with a natural user interface. It works on multiple platforms, including Windows, macOS,

Linux, iOS, and Android.

- **Features:**
  - Multi-touch support.
  - Declarative UI design using .kv files.
  - GPU-accelerated rendering.
- **Best For:** Cross-platform, touch-enabled applications.
- **Example:**

```python
from kivy.app import App
from kivy.uix.button import Button

class MyApp(App):
    def build(self):
        return Button(text="Hello, Kivy!")

MyApp().run()
```

## 4. wxPython

- **Description:**
  wxPython is a Python wrapper for the wxWidgets C
  ++ library, which allows developers to create native-
  looking desktop applications.
- **Features:**
  - Native look and feel on different platforms.
  - Rich set of pre-built widgets.
- **Best For:** Applications requiring a native OS
  appearance.
- **Example:**

```python
import wx

app = wx.App(False)
frame = wx.Frame(None, wx.ID_ANY, "wxPython
Example")
frame.Show(True)
app.MainLoop()
```

## 5. PyGTK

- **Description:**
  PyGTK is a set of Python wrappers for the GTK+ library, used for creating graphical interfaces.
- **Features:**
  - Designed for Linux environments but works on other platforms.
  - Strong community support.
- **Best For:** Applications targeted for GNOME-based systems.
- **Example:**

```
import gi
gi.require_version("Gtk", "3.0")
from gi.repository import Gtk

window = Gtk.Window(title="Hello PyGTK")
window.connect("destroy", Gtk.main_quit)
window.show_all()
Gtk.main()
```

## 6. Dear PyGui

- **Description:**
  Dear PyGui is a modern GUI framework with GPU-accelerated rendering, making it ideal for performance-intensive applications like visualization tools.
- **Features:**
  - High-performance rendering.
  - Easy-to-use API.
- **Best For:** Interactive and visually intensive applications.
- **Example:**

```
from dearpygui.core import *
from dearpygui.simple import *

def button_callback(sender, data):
    log_debug("Button Pressed!")

with window("Main Window"):
    add_button("Press Me", callback=button_callback)

start_dearpygui()
```

## 7. PyGame (for Game-like Interfaces)

- **Description:**
  PyGame is primarily a game development library but can be used to create interactive desktop apps with custom designs.

- **Features:**
    - Pixel-perfect control over UI.
    - Multimedia support (audio, video, and images).

- **Best For:** Applications requiring non-standard UI.

- **Example:**

```
import pygame

pygame.init()
screen = pygame.display.set_mode((400, 300))
pygame.display.set_caption("PyGame Example")

running = True
while running:
    for event in pygame.event.get():
        if event.type == pygame.QUIT:
            running = False
    screen.fill((255, 255, 255))
    pygame.display.flip()
```

```
pygame.quit()
```

## 8. Flexx

- **Description:**
  Flexx allows you to create desktop apps using Python and a web-based interface, leveraging HTML and JavaScript.

- **Features:**
  - Combines Python with web technologies.
  - Can run in a browser or as a standalone app.

- **Best For:** Web-like desktop applications.

- **Example:**

```
from flexx import app, ui

class ExampleApp(ui.Widget):
    def init(self):
        with ui.HBox():
            ui.Label(text="Hello, Flexx!")
            ui.Button(text="Click Me")

app.launch(ExampleApp)
app.run()
```

## 9. PySide6

- **Description:**
  PySide6 is the official Python module for the Qt library, offering the same features as PyQt but under a more permissive license.

- **Features:**

- ○ Modern UI elements and tools.
- ○ Cross-platform compatibility.
- **Best For:** Professional-grade applications.
- **Example:**

```
from PySide6.QtWidgets import QApplication, QLabel

app = QApplication([])
label = QLabel('Hello, PySide6!')
label.show()
   app.exec()
```

# CHAPTER 019: AN INTRODUCTION TO PYTHON DJANGO: THE FRAMEWORK FOR RAPID WEB DEVELOPMENT

Django, often referred to as "the web framework for perfectionists with deadlines," is a high-level Python web framework designed to make the process of building web applications faster and more efficient. It enables developers to focus on writing their application without having to reinvent the wheel.

In this article, we'll explore Django's features, architecture, and why it is one of the most popular web frameworks in the Python ecosystem.

## Why Choose Django?

Django is known for its simplicity and flexibility. Here are some of the key reasons developers choose Django:

1. **Batteries-Included Philosophy:** Django comes with a wide range of built-in features, such as an ORM (Object-Relational Mapper), admin panel, authentication system, and more, reducing the need for third-party libraries.

2. **Scalability:** It's designed to handle both small projects and large-scale applications with millions of users.

3. **Security:** Django provides robust security features, such as protection against SQL injection, cross-site scripting (XSS), cross-site request forgery (CSRF), and clickjacking.

4. **Community Support:** Django boasts a vibrant community that continuously updates the framework and provides extensive documentation and third-party packages.

5. **Rapid Development:** Its modular design and built-in tools enable quick prototyping and deployment of web applications.

## Key Features Of Django

### 1. Object-Relational Mapper (ORM):

Django's ORM allows developers to interact with databases using Python code instead of writing raw SQL. For example:

```
from myapp.models import Book

# Creating a new book entry
book = Book(title="Django for Beginners", author="John Doe")
book.save()
```

```
# Querying the database
books = Book.objects.filter(author="John Doe")
```

## 2. Built-in Admin Panel:

The admin interface is automatically generated for your models, providing a powerful way to manage data without additional coding.

```
# Run the following command to start the server
python manage.py runserver
```

Then, access the admin panel at http://127.0.0.1:8000/admin.

## 3. Template System:

Django's template engine helps separate business logic from presentation logic. A simple template might look like this:

```
<!DOCTYPE html>
<html>
<head>
    <title>{{ title }}</title>
</head>
<body>
    <h1>Welcome, {{ user.name }}!</h1>
</body>
</html>
```

## 4. URL Routing:

Django makes it easy to map URLs to views using its powerful URL dispatcher.

```
from django.urls import path
from . import views

urlpatterns = [
    path(", views.home, name='home'),
    path('about/', views.about, name='about'), ]
```

## 5. Middleware:

Middleware are hooks for processing requests and responses globally. Common middleware includes session management, authentication, and caching.

## Django's Architecture

Django follows the **Model-View-Template (MVT)** architectural pattern:

1. **Model:** Represents the data structure and handles the business logic. It defines the schema for your database.
2. **View:** Handles the logic that interacts with the model and prepares the data for rendering in the template.
3. **Template:** Displays data to the user in a presentable format.

## Getting Started with Django

Here's how to set up a basic Django project:

### Step 1: Install Django

First, ensure Python and pip are installed, then run:

```
pip install django
```

### Step 2: Create a New Project

```
django-admin startproject myproject
cd myproject
```

### Step 3: Create an App

```
python manage.py startapp myapp
```

### Step 4: Configure Your App

Add your app to the INSTALLED_APPS list in settings.py:

```
INSTALLED_APPS = [
    'myapp',
    'django.contrib.admin',
    'django.contrib.auth',
    'django.contrib.contenttypes',
```

```
    'django.contrib.sessions',
    'django.contrib.messages',
    'django.contrib.staticfiles',
]
```

## Step 5: Create Models

Define your data structure in models.py:

```python
from django.db import models

class Book(models.Model):
    title = models.CharField(max_length=100)
    author = models.CharField(max_length=50)
    published_date = models.DateField()

    def __str__(self):
        return self.title
```

## Step 6: Apply Migrations

```
python manage.py makemigrations
python manage.py migrate
```

## Step 7: Run the Server

```
python manage.py runserver
```

Access your project at http://127.0.0.1:8000/.

## Conclusion

*Django simplifies the process of web development with its robust features and intuitive design. Whether you're a beginner or an experienced developer, Django's versatility and efficiency make it a go-to framework for building modern web applications. With Django, you can spend less time on repetitive tasks and more time focusing on creating impactful applications.*

# CHAPTER 020
# MACHINE LEARNING USING PYTHON: A COMPREHENSIVE GUIDE

Machine Learning (ML) has revolutionized the way we interact with technology, enabling systems to learn and make decisions without being explicitly programmed. Python, with its simplicity and extensive libraries, has become the go-to programming language for machine learning practitioners. This article provides a detailed overview of machine learning using Python, covering key concepts, libraries, and a step-by-step implementation example.

## What is Machine Learning?

Machine learning is a subset of artificial intelligence (AI) that focuses on developing algorithms that allow computers to learn from and make predictions or decisions based on data. It is broadly categorized into three types:

1. **Supervised Learning**: The algorithm learns from labeled data, making predictions based on input-output pairs.
   - Examples: Regression, Classification
2. **Unsupervised Learning**: The algorithm identifies patterns and relationships in unlabeled data.
   - Examples: Clustering, Dimensionality Reduction
3. **Reinforcement Learning**: The algorithm learns by interacting with an environment to maximize rewards.
   - Examples: Game-playing AI, Robotics

## Why Python For Machine Learning?

Python is widely used for machine learning due to several reasons:

- **Ease of Use**: Python's simple syntax allows developers to focus on algorithms and data rather than the complexities of the language.
- **Rich Ecosystem**: Libraries like NumPy, Pandas, Scikit-learn, TensorFlow, and PyTorch simplify complex ML tasks.
- **Community Support**: A large community ensures robust support, extensive documentation, and pre-built solutions.

## Popular Python Libraries For Machine Learning

1. **NumPy**: Efficient handling of numerical data and operations.
2. **Pandas**: Data manipulation and analysis.

3. **Matplotlib & Seaborn**: Data visualization.

4. **Scikit-learn**: Comprehensive library for ML algorithms like regression, classification, and clustering.

5. **TensorFlow & Keras**: Deep learning frameworks for building neural networks.

6. **PyTorch**: Another powerful deep learning framework, especially popular in research.

7. **XGBoost**: Optimized library for gradient boosting.

## Understanding Key Statistical Concepts

1. **Mean, Median, Mode**:
   - **Mean**: The average value of a dataset.
   - **Median**: The middle value when the data is sorted.
   - **Mode**: The most frequently occurring value.

2. **Standard Deviation**: Measures the dispersion of data points from the mean. A low standard deviation indicates that data points are close to the mean, while a high standard deviation indicates a wide spread.

3. **Percentile**: Represents the value below which a percentage of data points fall. For example, the 90th percentile is the value below which 90% of the data lies.

4. **Data Distribution**: Understanding how data is distributed is crucial in ML. Common distributions include normal distribution, uniform distribution, and skewed distribution.

5. **Normal Data Distribution**: A bell-shaped curve where most data points are concentrated around the mean. Many ML algorithms assume data follows this distribution.

## Visualizing Data with Python

1. **Scatter Plot**: Useful for visualizing relationships between two variables.
2. import matplotlib.pyplot as plt
3. plt.scatter(X['RM'], y)
4. plt.xlabel('Number of Rooms')
5. plt.ylabel('House Price')
6. plt.show()
7. **Data Distribution Plots**:
8. import seaborn as sns
9. sns.histplot(data['MEDV'], kde=True)
10. plt.show()

## Regression Techniques

1. **Linear Regression**: Fits a straight line to the data to predict a target variable.
2. **Polynomial Regression**: Models non-linear relationships by fitting a polynomial curve.
3. **Multiple Regression**: Extends linear regression to include multiple independent variables.
4. **Logistic Regression**: Used for binary classification tasks, predicting probabilities between 0 and 1.

## Scaling and Splitting Data

1. **Scaling**: Ensures all features have comparable ranges. Popular methods include standard scaling and min-max scaling.
2. from sklearn.preprocessing import StandardScaler
3. scaler = StandardScaler()
4. X_scaled = scaler.fit_transform(X)
5. **Train/Test Split**: Divides data into training and

testing sets.

6. from sklearn.model_selection import train_test_split
7. X_train, X_test, y_train, y_test = train_test_split(X, y, test_size=0.2, random_state=42)

## Advanced Machine Learning Techniques

1. **Decision Tree**: A tree-like model used for classification and regression tasks.

2. **Confusion Matrix**: Evaluates classification models by showing true positives, true negatives, false positives, and false negatives.

3. from sklearn.metrics import confusion_matrix
4. cm = confusion_matrix(y_test, y_pred)
5. print(cm)

6. **Hierarchical Clustering**: Groups data into a hierarchy of clusters.

7. **K-Means Clustering**: Partitions data into K distinct clusters.

8. from sklearn.cluster import KMeans
9. kmeans = KMeans(n_clusters=3)
10. kmeans.fit(X)

11. **K-Nearest Neighbors (KNN)**: A simple, instance-based learning algorithm used for classification.

12. **Cross Validation**: Evaluates models by splitting data into multiple folds.

13. **Grid Search**: Optimizes hyper parameters by searching across a predefined grid of parameters.

14. from sklearn.model_selection import GridSearchCV
15. grid_search = GridSearchCV(model, param_grid={'alpha': [0.1, 1, 10]}, cv=5)
16. grid_search.fit(X_train, y_train)

17. **AUC-ROC Curve**: Measures the performance of classification models at various threshold settings.

```
18. from sklearn.metrics import roc_auc_score
19. auc = roc_auc_score(y_test, y_pred)
20. print(f"AUC: {auc}")
```

*Python's extensive ecosystem and user-friendly nature make it an ideal choice for machine learning. Whether you are a beginner or an experienced practitioner, Python provides all the tools necessary to build, train, and deploy machine learning models effectively. With continuous learning and practice, you can harness the power of machine learning to solve real-world problems.*

# CONCLUSION

Congratulations on completing this journey through Python programming! You've unlocked the power of code and built a strong foundation in one of the most versatile and widely used programming languages. Let's reflect on what you've accomplished and explore the exciting path ahead.

## *Wrapping Up*

- **Recap of What You've Learned**

Throughout this book, you have explored:

- **Python Basics** : Variables, data types, and control structures.
- **Functions and Reusability** : Writing efficient and modular code.
- **Data Structures** : Handling lists, dictionaries, and more.
- **File Handling** : Reading, writing, and working with CSV and JSON files.
- **APIs and Libraries** : Connecting your code to the world and utilizing powerful tools.
- **Object-Oriented Programming** : Designing scalable and reusable code with classes and objects.

- **Visualization and Automation** : Bringing data to life and simplifying repetitive tasks.

- **Python Modules**: Using built-in and custom modules to organize and reuse code efficiently (e.g., math, os, sys).

- **Math Functions**: Performing complex mathematical operations using the math module (e.g., trigonometric functions, logarithms, factorials).

- **Date Functions**: Managing dates and times using the datetime module, including formatting and arithmetic on dates.

- **Introduction to MongoDB**: Overview of NoSQL databases and MongoDB's document-oriented model.

- **CRUD Operations**: Creating, reading, updating, and deleting data in MongoDB collections using Python.

- **Indexing and Aggregation**: Enhancing query performance and analysing data effectively.

- **Connection and Integration**: Using libraries like PyMongo to connect Python applications to MongoDB.

- **Connecting Python with MySQL**: Establishing a connection using mysql.connector or SQLAlchemy.

- **Executing SQL Queries:** Performing SELECT, INSERT, UPDATE, and DELETE operations with Python.

- **Error Handling:** Managing database exceptions gracefully in Python scripts.

- **Data Security:** Using parameterized queries to prevent SQL injection attacks.

  - **Flask**: A lightweight framework for building APIs and small-scale web applications.

  - **FastAPI**: A modern framework for creating fast and scalable APIs with built-in validation.

  - **Tkinter**: Developing desktop GUI applications in

Python.

- **PyQt/PySide**: Advanced GUI frameworks for building professional desktop applications.

- **Introduction to Django**: Overview of Django's MVC architecture and its "batteries included" philosophy.

- **Creating Models**: Defining database structures with Django ORM.

- **Developing Views and Templates**: Linking backend logic with user-friendly interfaces.

- **Authentication and Security**: Implementing user authentication and protecting web applications.

- **Django REST Framework**: Building RESTful APIs for web services.

- **Introduction to ML Concepts**: Understanding supervised, unsupervised, and reinforcement learning.

- **Data Preprocessing**: Cleaning and preparing data for analysis with libraries like Pandas and NumPy.

- **Model Training and Evaluation**: Using Scikit-learn for regression, classification, and clustering models.

- **Deep Learning with TensorFlow/Keras**: Building and training neural networks for advanced ML tasks.

- **Visualization and Interpretation**: Analyzing ML results with tools like Matplotlib and Seaborn.

From solving mathematical puzzles to building real-world projects, you've covered an incredible range of topics that demonstrate Python's versatility.

## Encouragement For Further Exploration

This is just the beginning! Python offers countless opportunities to grow as a programmer. Whether you're interested in data science, web development, artificial intelligence, or game design, Python is your gateway to success. Every concept you've learned here will serve as a stepping stone for future projects.

## Next Steps In Your Python Journey:

**1. Experiment with Projects** : Start small, like creating a to-do list app, and gradually tackle bigger challenges like a web scraper or a chatbot.

**2. Deepen Your Knowledge** : Explore advanced Python topics such as decorators, generators, and multi-threading.

**3. Learn Complementary Skills** : Delve into frameworks like Flask or Django for web development, or explore machine learning with libraries like TensorFlow.

**4. Collaborate and Share** : Join online communities to collaborate on open-source projects, participate in hackathons, and share your work.

- **Exercise: Reflect on Your Favourite Part**

Write a short Python script that showcases your favourite topic from the book. For example, create a small program using APIs or visualize data using matplotlib.

## Bonus Resources:

### Recommended Books, Courses, and Websites

- **Books :** Automate the Boring Stuff with Python by Al Sweigart, Python Crash Course by Eric Matthes.
- **Online Courses** : Check out Python tutorials on Coursera, Udemy, or Codecademy.
- **Websites** : Explore Python documentation, Real Python, and GeeksforGeeks for in-depth guides and tutorials.

## Community And Forums To Join

- **Reddit** : r/Python for discussions and tips.
- **Stack Overflow** : Get help with coding problems.
- **GitHub** : Discover and contribute to open-source projects.

## Additional Project Ideas

- Create a personal finance tracker.
- Build a weather dashboard using APIs.
- Develop a simple game like Tic Tac Toe or Hangman.
- Automate tasks like organizing your desktop files or sending emails.

---

**Exercise: Join a Community**
Sign up for an online coding community or forum.
Share one of your projects and get feedback from other programmers

---

## Appendix

- Cheat Sheets for Python Syntax and Functions
- Keep a handy reference for common Python commands, functions, and libraries.

## End Note

*Python Magic: Turn Ideas into Code with Ease was written to help you discover how programming can transform your creativity into reality. From automating mundane tasks to building exciting projects, Python*

PYTHON PROGRAMMING LANGUAGE

*empowers you to make your ideas come to life. The journey doesn't end here it's a stepping stone to endless opportunities.*

Happy coding, and may your Python journey be as adventurous and rewarding as the magic you've created along the way!

www.ingramcontent.com/pod-product-compliance
Lightning Source LLC
LaVergne TN
LVHW051334050326
832903LV00031B/3528